KEY WEST
THE TRUTH ALWAYS HAS CONSEQUENCES

Copyright © 2013 by Peter Wick

All rights reserved.

ISBN-13: 978-0-692-30257-6

Some names and identifying details have been changed to protect the privacy of individuals.

This book or any portion thereof may not be reproduced or used in any manner whatsoever without the express written permission of the publisher except for the use of brief quotations in a book review.

First Printing, 2013

Printed in the United States of America

Contents

From the Author 5
Disclaimers 7
Offshore gambling 9
Grand Jury 13
Doing this for Bill Lee 18
Things you can count on 22
Orange rooster 30
We have a couple problems 33
Shut down 41
Witch hunt 47
We're not going to kill you 48
A walking message 52
MURPHY 54
The man with the bucket of fish 61
The good stuff 66
Ask a man what he's angry about 73
A Florida story 79
Intimidation and Benevolence 82
It's empty 84
May he always land on his ass 86
It's a story, not a STORY 89
Of course you're right 92
I might be a dead woman 94
Absolute power 99
Raised in the ways of righteousness 100
Knocking on doors 105
Expected better from you 108

Hooking the shark 110
Bring Trumbull down 113
Beat him at his own game 116
You and me 122
Change of plans 126
Damn good newspapermen 132
The rest of the story 134
About The Author: 137

FROM THE AUTHOR

KEY WEST, is based in part on my good friend Robert Silk's 2007 *Key West Magazine* article, "Wanna bet?"

The story also benefits from extensive additional research by Robert Silk. I want to take this moment to thank Mr. Silk for his hard work, patience, and enduring support. In keeping with the spirit of this story, I have even lost a few odd bets to him involving Manchester United and Italian giants, Juventus.

Disclaimers

While inspired by real events and characters, this story has been fictionalized for dramatic effect.

Additional materials used in the shaping of this story include a piece written by former Miami Herald reporter, Pat Murphy, in the year 2000 for the Idaho Mountain Express, in which he observed and characterized State Representative Bernie Papy's relationship with Key West in the 1950's as a "fiefdom." Also from this Murphy piece, the author has borrowed the phrase "Intimidation and benevolence," which is used in Trumbull's fictionalized newspaper column on page 63.

While Stephen Trumbull's column was, in fact, titled, "Dear Cuz," all representations of the column in this novel are fictionalized by the Author, with the exception of the aforementioned use of the words "Fiefdom," and "intimidation and benevolence," which the author openly borrows from Trumbull's colleague, Pat Murphy.

OFFSHORE GAMBLING

Trumbull would have found it funny; three clueless tourists going out in the hurricane of the decade, to lose all their money on an offshore gambling boat.

If Trumbull was still around he would have downed a swig of good single-malt scotch and smiled a rare smile.

He almost never smiled. When he did it was always accompanied by a scotch.

But Trumbull was long gone. Trumbull's piercing gaze, his relentless search for the truth, his newspaper column, "Dear Cuz," his ability to read a person, to read a person's intentions, to read a person's bullshit, Trumbull's friends...his enemies, they were all long gone.

That story: in a moment.

First: those three clueless tourists.

It was Hurricane Wilma, 2005. John was the ring leader. You know the type; thinks it's a sign of weakness to back down from danger. Maybe Donnie was the sensible one. He wasn't sure about going. Bill always went along with John. He needed John's approval.

So there they were, boarding a charter boat to take them three miles off shore to The Lady Luck.

Hurricane Wilma was serious. Buildings were being torn apart. Rain was coming down like bullets. Not really coming down so much as flying sideways. The Captain of the charter boat knew better, but he needed the money, so he pulled away from the dock just hoping, hoping he would make it back. He knew what the guys didn't know; this could be their swan song.

"It's really coming down," John said, happy with that sick happiness you get when adrenaline has clouded your judgment.

"Are you sure this is a good idea?" Donnie asked.

""Stop whining, Donnie," John said.

"Just don't get sick in THIS boat," Bill said

"Yeah, at least wait until we get out there," John added.

"How far is it?"

"Three miles," John said, for the fifteenth time.

"Three miles?!"

"Yes, Donnie," said Bill.

"Why so far?"

Bill sighed and took a breath. "We've been through this." He looked at John and they rolled eyes together. "Can you explain this to him?"

So once again John tried to make Donnie understand that gambling was illegal unless you traveled at least three miles offshore, that The Lady Luck was a great experience, that he had won a couple grand last time, that is to say he won it before he lost it again, and if only he hadn't made that last bet.

But the boys had bigger things to worry about than making one bet too many. Or to be more precise, they had already made one bet too many.

The Miami Herald Office in 2005 didn't have much of the flavor Trumbull would have remembered from 1950. It was a good newspaper office, though, and Trumbull would have been proud of the way they were working the hurricane.

Nothing beats the controlled chaos of a newsroom trying to get their paragraphs around a real-time disaster.

Phones ringing, people yelling, an editor taking it all in, barking out instantaneous decisions.

"It's pounding the Keys!"

"Yeah? Yeah? Wait Where'd – damn phone's dead!"

"Markham, Sterling's in Key West. Try him."

"I've got Sterling, on the phone with him now."

"You have him!?"

"Gambling boats! We have gambling boats out."

"In this!?"

"The Lady Luck - The Paradise."

And in the middle of the chaos a brief black-out. Nothing. Silence.

"Uh oh."

"Come on. Come on!"

And after a few long second the lights were back on.

"Hello? Sterling?"

"Lose him?"

"Hello, Hi – no he's here."

"Tell him to get the story but stay safe."

"Hey - Hey, Sterling, get the story but don't freakin' die!"

The three boys and their charter boat had reached the Lady Luck. Donnie was paying the price. The waves, the rocking, the boat being tossed around in the hurricane like a toy, all combined to make Donnie regret eating anything. He was leaning off the side of the boat, holding onto a guard rail for dear life, giving up his stomach's contents to the sea.

"Donnie," John said, shaking his head, "you are embarrassing."

"Please, make it stop," Donnie said. "Please someone stop rocking the boat."

And then suddenly the wind, the rain, the forces of nature that every sane person fears, came down from the heavens and threw both boats into each other. It was the last thing any of them would ever know.

By morning large broken pieces of The Lady Luck were floating calmly, peacefully, in open calm waters. The charter boat was a distant memory, torn to pieces so small no one would ever be able to accurately identify them.

The Lady Luck would make it to a Herald headline, though not for the reasons anyone wants to be in newspaper headline.

For Nature, it was just another day at the office.

As for John, and his fear of weakness in the face of danger, I suppose you could say he was weak. Everyone is.

GRAND JURY

The eyes of the nation were on a modest county court building tucked away in a modest corner of town, that morning in 1950.

Everyone just assumed Papy would be indicted; Representative Bernie Papy, to be clear. Papy represented Monroe County in the Florida State Legislature. Key West. It was an open secret in 1950 that if you wanted anything that wasn't quite legal, you could find it in Key West. Gambling, cockfights, fixed boxing matches, whores.

A year earlier, in 1949, a reporter named Bill Lee started poking around, nosing into things that the locals wanted to keep under wraps.

His body was found in an alley with a copy of his latest news story stuffed into his mouth. The message, most people figured, was that he was eating his words.

The murder kicked off a half-serious attempt to prove that Papy ran Key West, and had his fingers in a dozen different illegal activities.

Now, a year later, with the eyes of the nation watching, a Grand Jury was reading its decision.

Trumbull was angry, but not surprised.

The door of the court room opened and the herd of reporters streamed out like cattle let out of a gate that had been closed for too long. They beat each other to the wall of phones to call in their reports.

Trumbull and Murphy came out last. Murphy would have been part of the stampede, but he thought he should wait for Trumbull, and Trumbull just sat for a while. When they did come out, Trumbull looked at the wild herd of reporters yapping into phones, and looked down at the floor.

Murphy didn't move. Finally Trumbull looked at him and said, "That report isn't going to call itself in."

Murphy nodded and went to the last open wall phone. As Murphy dialed, Trumbull pushed his hat up off his eyes and looked out through the glass doors of the building, out into the street, where the locals were going on about their lives as if everything was fine.

He listened as Murphy began that excited monotone unique to newspapermen; "This is Murphy, Key West. Ready? A Monroe County Grand Jury failed, today, to prove the existence of illegal gambling in Key West. Stop. The investigation began a year ago, in the wake of the murder of local reporter Bill Lee. It concluded today –"

Trumbull stopped listening. He figured Murphy would get it right, get the facts. He was on to something deeper.

Looking through those glass doors, he wondered what the real Key West was. He saw a small group of Cuban kids kicking a soccer ball in the street, expertly dodging traffic as they played. Across the street was another group of kids, a little older, rolling dice against a stoop. Down the block from them a woman, dressed suggestively in a tight red dress, led a mouse-y looking man into a run-down house. He wasn't sure what to make of it all yet.

Then Murphy's monotone brought him back to the moment; "-Released a statement that says, quote, 'The Grand jury is not prepared to state unequivocally that there is no gambling in Monroe County. If there is such gambling, the citizenry of this county is apparently unwilling to present evidence."

And then a loud squeal of microphone feedback brought the entire room to a halt.

A technician was setting up a live microphone against the wall. "Test test," rang through the room as he tapped the mic and got the feedback to stop.

Then, there he was, Papy. He was standing off to the side of the room, waiting for the microphone to be ready. He had his hands in his pockets, in a cocky manner that annoyed Trumbull as soon as he saw it. The bastard got away with it, and now he was going to gloat. Worse, he was going to play victim.

Unknown to Papy, though, the microphone was already on, and picked up a piece of conversation between Papy and a nervous looking man named Prescott. They were whispering, at first, Prescott pressing an envelope into Papy's hand. "Not right now, Prescott," Papy said, clearly audible throughout the room.

"It's – it's um – "

"I'm – Prescott, I'm – there are reporters here!"

Prescott and Papy realized at the same moment that the entire room was listening to them. "Oh, okay," Prescott said. "It's – it's," and Prescott leaned in and whispered something into Papy's ear that annoyed Papy noticeably.

"The hell it is!" Papy said, before gathering himself together and putting his pleasant-face back on. Papy quickly grabbed the envelope from Prescott and faced the room full of reporters.

"Thank you. Good afternoon. Hello," he said, clearing his throat. "Gentlemen, as the duly elected representative of my people, the great people of Monroe County, let me take this opportunity to congratulate the grand jury on exonerating the great citizens of this county today."

The sea of reporters opened fire. "Representative Papy- Was the verdict truly? - How do you respond to the allegations of corruption?"

"Gentlemen, gentlemen," Papy said, gaining control of the room, "The Grand Jury has spoken. Now I must get back to doing the work of my people."

Trumbull couldn't hold himself back any longer. "How much did you win?" he barked out.

A silence came over the crowd of reporters. Papy turned to Trumbull. The two men knew each other, but until now had kept their distance from each other. Now their eyes were locked.

"Gentlemen," Papy said. "I'm sure you recognize Stephen Trumbull of the Miami Herald a man who lives for slander and unproven innuendo, a man who loves to rock the boat. I'm sorry, Mr. Trumbull, was there a question?"

"This was a hell of a case, Papy," Trumbull said, taking control of the room back from Papy. "Big, big case, dead reporter, big investigation, grand jury, the eyes of the whole country on you. A lot was riding on this."

"I still, Mr. Trumbull, have not heard a question.'

"You placed a bet on the outcome," Trumbull bluffed. Trumbull was a master at bluffing. He considered it a priceless skill to nurture and develop. "How much were your winnings?"

Prescott, a man two or three I.Q. points lower than the ideal, blurted from nearby, "How....how did you know all that?"

"I didn't, Prescott, but I do now. Thanks for confirming." Trumbull jotted something into his notepad, and stuffed it into his coat pocket with a wry smirk.

Papy was livid. Papy eyed Prescott with a seething anger that no one present could have missed.

DOING THIS FOR BILL LEE

"Is this your way of separating business from personal?'

Lee Hills, Miami Herald Editor, was sitting, leaning, against the front of his desk, in a casual manner that masked the seriousness he held for his job. Trumbull eyed him with respect.

"It's not personal," Trumbull said.

"You're like kids, the two of you. It's a damn playground brawl."

"I'm right, Hills. You know I'm right."

Hills took a moment before responding. He was used to these arguments with Trumbull, and yes, Trumbull was almost always right. He just had a way of saying things that rubbed people the wrong way.

It made for good reading, though, and his "Dear Cuz" column was the star column of the paper. Over the years Hills had developed this careful dance with Trumbull. He cautioned Trumbull to go easy on some issues. Trumbull ignored him. They respected each other. Life went on.

"You are right," Hills said.

"Nice of you to say so."

"It would be nice if we could follow journalistic standards, though."

"I follow standards," Trumbull said.

Hills smirked. He knew this argument was a lost cause. It was alright. He knew Trumbull would dig up something big. He just had to try to keep him focused. "You follow standards..."

"By the book,' Trumbull said confidently.

"Which book?"

"Papy gets away with murder, literally."

Hills moved back to the chair behind his desk. His hope now was just to massage Trumbull a little, keep him from crossing the line in going after Papy. "Listen, Trumbull, we both know how popular your column is."

"We've done well by each other Hills."

"You write gripping stuff."

"What's your point?"

"Dig deeper, Trumbull," Hills said. "Goddammit, be a journalist. Make sure everything is backed up."

"I'm going to Key West," Trumbull said.

"Would it do any good to remind you how this started?"

"No."

"Bill Lee – " Hills trailed off.

Trumbull leaned forward. "I'm doing this for Bill Lee."

"He started snooping around, stepping on the wrong toes."

"The right toes." Trumbull was quiet but forceful.

Hills looked across the desk at him. "It got him killed," he said matter-of-factly.

"So someone has to pick up where he left off."

Hills was quiet. He shuffled some papers on his desk. He took a deep breath. He looked up. "Go to Key West."

"That's all I'm asking for."

"I would tell you to keep your head down, but-'

"Don't worry about me," Trumbull said.

"I worry. It's part of my job."

"I'll see you in a few weeks." Trumbull stood up, and walked toward the door.

Hills watched him go. He shook his head. Then he smiled.

Out in the newsroom, Murphy and the others watched Trumbull go to his desk to gather his things. They held Trumbull up as a hero, but they tried not to make a show of it. Trumbull didn't care much for hero worship.

He picked up his bulky typewriter and fitted it into its carrying case. He collected some papers. From a few desks away Murphy quietly said, "Go get 'em, Trumbull."

"See you in a few weeks, Murphy," Trumbull said without looking up.

Trumbull opened the top drawer of his desk and pulled out his .45 caliber hand gun.

"Trumbull..." Murphy couldn't process the right words, so he just stopped.

"Is there a question, Murphy?"

"You're a journalist. Your weapon is a pen."

"You ever try using a pen as a weapon, Murphy?"

"All the time."

"Is this where you tell me the pen is mightier than the sword?"

"It's silly, but it's true," Murphy said.

"You need them both, Murphy. The pen is a weapon. It needs back-up, though. Bill Lee could have used some back-up. You see, Murphy, on a story like this, a pen and a gun are a damn good combination. Like a flask, and good scotch." As Trumbull said it he unscrewed the top from his flask and tipped it back. He rubbed his mouth with the sleeve of his overcoat, and smiled at Murphy.

Murphy smiled back. Then he watched as Trumbull carried his things out the door.

The drive out to Key West was quiet and peaceful. Trumbull watched the natural beauty pass by as he drove. Ironic, he thought, that some of the most twisted, corrupt places are nestled into the most beautiful surroundings. He looked out at the unending expanse of water. There's good fishing out here. Further out Is Cuba. Hemingway wouldn't be around Key West anymore. He had moved to Cuba. Trumbull focused back on the road and drove.

THINGS YOU CAN COUNT ON

"Dear Cuz;
I met Bill Lee three years ago. He was a good man, a newspaper man, cared about the truth.

It's a dangerous thing to care about the truth in Key West. It can get you killed.

A year ago the truth got Bill Lee killed.

Last week the grand jury decided that the truth may as well be buried along with him.

I came to Key West to find the illegal gambling that the grand jury winked at. It's not hard to find.

I asked a local policeman - one of Key West's finest - Police Chief Martins. Turns out, Chief Martins was very helpful.

You see, Cuz, it isn't the gambling I have a problem with. It's the hypocrisy and corruption."

Trumbull sat in a modest hotel room with his clothes and papers spread out in a display of clutter on the bed behind him. He had the typewriter set up on the desk facing the window. He typed quickly and with purpose, trying to capture the impromptu meeting he'd had with Martins earlier.

Trumbull knew he was headed for The Boat Bar on Duval Street. It was the worst kept secret in Key West. There were other places. Slots were out in the open at several bars around town, but The Boat Bar was the hub. Everyone knew it. When Trumbull spotted Martins' uniform, though, he decided to have a little fun.

"Evening," the police chief said, as he saw Trumbull walking toward him.

"Good evening." Trumbull poked the brim of his hat up, giving him a slightly comical look.

"Visitor?"

"You got me," Trumbull said. "On vacation from Atlanta."

"Well, welcome to Key West."

"Say, I was wondering-" Trumbull was fully into character.

"Yes?"

"A friend of mine told me I could find a little action around here.

The police chief didn't hesitate. "What are you looking for? Roulette? Poker?"

"I'm a decent poker hand," Trumbull said.

"The Boat Bar," Martins said, pointing down Duval Street. "Right over there. Watch out for Barnes, though," he added, casually. "He'll take the shirt off your back.'

"Much obliged."

Trumbull poked the brim of his hat again and walked away. As he approached the Boat bar, though, he put his hat down over his eyes. No sense in being too noticeable, he thought. The most comical part of that exchange was that Martins didn't recognize him. Trumbull knew who Martins was, though. Scenes like that don't exactly raise your opinion of the human race.

The Boat Bar was a clatter of noise. As Trumbull walked in, a group of people were cheering a roulette spin to the right of the entranceway. To the left, a large round table hosted a poker game. Along the walls rows of slots dinged and clattered. Trumbull watched the poor and the misguided throw their money into the rigged slot machines. They were always surprised and disappointed when they didn't win, and they always fished around for whatever change they could throw away on the next pull.

Trumbull sauntered casually through the room trying not to draw attention to himself. He sat on a bar stool.

"Scotch on the rocks," he told the bartender.

As the bartender prepared the drink, Trumbull leaned his back against the bar and looked at the scene playing out in front of him. He eyed the poker game. He squinted, spotting something even that far away that didn't look right.

Trumbull had failed at not drawing attention to himself. Before he knew it, a woman was sitting next to him. She was beautiful in that way most women aren't. She might have been 35 or even 40. She had a few lines on her face. They looked good to Trumbull. He had often told Murphy, "Never trust someone who doesn't have a few lines on their face. Man or woman, doesn't matter. If a person's face has no lines, no signs of life, no sign that the person has seen a thing or two, get out. Leave."

"Looking for something in particular?" she asked.

Trumbull eyed her and kept quiet. She waited. What game is she playing, he asked himself. He had grown weary of these games.

"Nope," he finally said.

She extended her hand to him. "Eva," she said.

He looked at the hand.

Trumbull always tried to tell himself he was through with women. He knew it was a lie, the only thing he ever lied to himself about.

Finally he reached out to her hand. He shook it. The contact sent a chill through him. "What's your line of work, Eva?" he asked.

"I'm an entertainer," she said.

"Really, and what line of entertainment are you in?"

But she didn't have a chance to answer. A loud commotion erupted from the poker table.

"Show your cards!" a man said, rising up from his seat.

"Sit down!" another man said.

"Stand up and lay your cards on the table!"

A third man, sitting with cards hidden behind his own palm looked over at the accused. "Bad move," the third man said. "Bad bad move!"

"You are a goddamn cheater," the first man said. "You are a sorry-ass goddamn cheater!"

The accused finally rose from his seat, indignant, and said, "What did you just call me?"

His accuser reached over and grabbed the cards out of his hand. "Cheater! Look, marked cards! Marked, goddamn cards!"

"Give me those –"

And a scuffle began that saw most of the chips on the poker table knocked onto the floor. The two men, plus the other players, engaged in a chaotic back and forth that no one would win.

Into this scene, walked a gentleman in a suit and hat. Everyone knew him as Walter. Walter kept things like this from getting out of control. He was calm, cool, collected, and dangerous.

"Alright, alright, what's the problem here?" Walter shouted, pulling the two men apart.

"See for yourself. Marked cards," the accuser sputtered.

"I don't know what he's talking about," the accused yelled. "I'm playing as honest as the day is long.'

Walter took the cards and inspected them. He turned his head toward the other end of the room and nodded.

Two young toughs came over from where Walter had nodded. They were brutish men, maybe Cuban, maybe Jamaican. They had the look of young men who had survived by sheer strength, goons, really. They had lived to see today, while others they knew hadn't. They clearly had a trail of blood in their pasts. It was written on their faces.

"This man," Walter said calmly, pausing for effect, "has been cheating at cards." He looked at the two goons. "This is the second time he has been caught." Another pregnant silence held the room. "Escort him out back."

Without saying anything, the goons grabbed the cheater.

"Hey let go – dirty bastards! Let go of me!"

And the door to the back alley slammed shut behind them.

Trumbull took a drink.

A loud, pain-filled shriek came from the back alley. Then it was quiet.

Walter stepped into the middle of the room and announced, "I apologize, everyone. Please enjoy one free drink, everyone, one drink on the house. Thank you." He met eyes with the bartender, and the two nodded at each other.

Slowly the atmosphere returned to normal. The slots began dinging and clattering again. The roulette wheel spun. Trumbull took another drink and looked over at the poker table. Eva was still sitting next to him.

"The funny thing is," Trumbull said to her, "that guy wasn't the only one cheating at the table."

"No?"

"He was just the dumbest guy cheating at the table."

"Really? Who else?" she asked.

But once again they were interrupted, this time for good, as a stream of sailors from the nearby Navy base poured in the front door, bringing noise and mayhem in with them.

"Woohoo! — Beer all around! — How much to buy into this poker game?"

Trumbull turned to Eva, and shouted to be heard; "America's finest!" he said.

"I forgot it was the fifteenth," she said.

"What's special about the fifteenth?"

"There are three things you can count on in Key West," she shouted.

"Just three?"

"One, you can always count on a good time. Two, the first and fifteenth of every month the sailors from Boca Chica Naval Station put their government paychecks to very good use."

Eva got up and began to walk away.

"What's the third thing?" Trumbull shouted after her.

She turned back seductively, swinging her hips back and forth to the Latino music that had begun pounding throughout the bar, and burned her eyes into him. "The third is ME," she shouted back. "You can always count on me."

"Count on you for what?" But by the time Trumbull had finished the question, Eva was surrounded by several dancing sailors.

Trumbull finished his scotch and shook his head.

He bided his time. He had seen enough of the Boat Bar for tonight. He would be back. For now he waited until he was sure no one was paying attention, and then he slipped out the back door.

He stepped into the dark alley cautiously. The beam from a streetlight angled into the alley, dimly lighting about half of it. As he looked down to his left, he saw him, the lifeless body of the dumbest cheater at the poker table. Trumbull moved toward the body. He wasn't sure why, exactly. It was clear he was dead. Trumbull reached down to the body's jacket. He pulled the jacket open. The knife wound stretched across the man's stomach. It was deep, intending to kill. Just to be sure, the goons had cut his neck as well. Blood soaked the man's shirt and dripped onto the pavement.

Trumbull stood and lingered over the dead body for a minute. He looked around, took in a deep breath of the alley's foul-smelling garbage-filled air. He walked to the end of the alley and stopped before walking out into the street. He pulled his hat down and peered around the corner of the building — looked clear. He walked out into the street, and quickly onto a side street.

Back in his hotel room Trumbull took a swig from his flask, and sat in the chair facing the typewriter. It was late, but he had a lot to sort through, not the least of which were his personal demons.

He sat thinking about Eva. He didn't want to. Women were nothing but a problem, he thought. Why does someone like her have to come along and spoil his focus? He couldn't get her out of his mind. Then his thoughts drifted back to years earlier, to his time with Sarah, the happy times. He wanted to remember the happy times, but then came the memories of the end. It was a package deal. If he wanted to remember the good times, there was also no escaping the way it ended. Trumbull took another drink and shifted the blank piece of paper in the typewriter.

Writing is one the few honest professions, he felt, but so many people did it so wrong. They don't have any life to write about. Just sit around indoors with nothing to write about but girlfriends and their own ego. You have to go out and face a little danger.

These running dialogues went on inside his head all the time.

He took another drink.

That brought up the memory of his Dad.

One more drink to push that thought out. He pulled the chair up to the desk, and forced himself to begin typing.

ORANGE ROOSTER

Trumbull woke up late. The sun poured in through the window and refused to let him sleep.

He had work to do.

After a quick breakfast and coffee, he headed out to find what he could. It didn't take long. On the edge of town, he heard an excited crowd. He followed the noise and found a large group of men, forty, maybe more, including a dozen or more of last night's sailors, circled around an outdoor cock-fighting pit.

Moving into the crowd he saw the roosters, jabbing at each other, squawking, egged on by the wild crowd.

There was a black rooster and an orange rooster. The orange one had already gotten the best of the black one. The black rooster's left wing hung lifelessly to its side.

The black rooster had a lot of will to live, though, so it kept at it. It bobbed and pecked like a boxer. Trumbull had heard that you could read a rooster's personality just like you can read a person's.

That black rooster had a lot of drive. It also had a lot of supporters in the crowd. Each time it took a dive into the orange rooster's neck, half the crowd erupted. It did its best, but the orange rooster had its number. After a few near misses, the orange one went in for the kill.

It wasn't pretty.

The half-dead black rooster kept trying to do something. Only half its body was responding, so it kept moving in a half-circle, until it just slowed to a stop. Even the orange rooster, the victorious bird, was in no shape to celebrate. Half bloody, it wandered aimlessly for a while, squawking half-heartedly, like a playground fighter who has just had the life knocked out of him, but gave even worse, and is now strutting around slurring trash-talk that no one can take seriously.

After the crowd of men quieted down, half of them went to a man at the back of a row of make-shift seats, where they collected their winnings. Then things got really interesting. Maybe one man thought he bet on the orange one, but didn't, or said he did, and hoped no one was keeping track.

A fight broke out.

Trumbull found it amusing. Apparently watching the roosters didn't satisfy them. They had to act like damn roosters themselves.

Trumbull noticed that Police Chief Martins was standing nearby, counting his own winnings. Martins was ignoring the fight trying quietly to get away from it.

"Hey," Martins said, "Vacation-from-Atlanta, how's the visit going?"

Trumbull poked his hat up. "Well, I'm still here," he said. "More than I can say for that bird.'

Martins laughed. "Great. Well if there's anything you need, we're here to help."

Before Trumbull could speak again, a series of real blows were landed on the man who claimed he'd won but hadn't. The man's friends were firing back. The scene was quickly descending into primitive anarchy.

"I'm sure you'll be very helpful," Trumbull said.

Martins got a whiff of the sarcasm and turned around. "Yes, these guys do make a habit of this. Hey, now, Hey! What's going on here!?"

And Trumbull was free to drop his vacation-from-Atlanta character.

He walked away. He wasn't sure where he was going. He just walked. He knew he was looking for something. He wouldn't know what until he found it.

Down the street, a group of people were gathered around a man speaking Spanish.

"Bolita! Bolita boletas! Aqui! Aqui!"

The crowd of people pressed in. This crowd was different from the one gathered around the unfortunate roosters. It included women, a few children. Everyone spoke Spanish. The man at the center was taking money from the people, and handing back tickets.

Trumbull didn't stay to watch the crowd. His attention was drawn down the street to two men in a doorway, surreptitiously exchanging money.

And then the orange rooster wandered by. It seemed lost. It walked as if it were drunk. It let out a drunken squawk as it wandered — then a second squawk. Trumbull looked back down the street to see if anyone from the cockfighting pit was interested in taking care of the winning rooster.

No one seemed interested.

WE HAVE A COUPLE PROBLEMS

Papy had a swagger to him.

He climbed the steps to the State Capital building in Tallahassee like a king ascending to his throne. He burst through the door expecting his aide, Davis to be waiting for him, and just about every morning, Davis was right there.

"Morning Davis.'

"Good morning."

"What's on for today? What's my schedule?"

Davis, the always-efficient aide, flipped a page in a small pocket-sized notebook and coughed. That was when Papy knew it wasn't good news. Papy and Davis had been doing this for years, and Papy knew every tick, every cough, every throat-clearing move Davis had. Still he was the best, most organized side man Papy had ever known.

"I have news you might not like."

Papy also loved Davis for not beating around the bush. Just say it. Davis was always direct.

"Spill it," Papy said, matter-of-factly.

"First, it looks like Representative Matheson, from Palm Beach, is introducing legislation to regulate bookies."

"Regulate bookies? Again!?'

"I don't know when he's introducing it. Not today. Later this week."

Papy rolled his eyes. "Goddamn it!"

"Word is-"

"Didn't we just kill this?" Papy said, speeding up his pace as they walked through the hallway. "Three months convincing Watson to drop his."

"Yes," Davis said, waiting for his chance to move on to the bigger problem.

"Representative who? Matheson?"

"Matheson, yes," Davis said.

"Who the hell is he?"

"New. Just elected."

Papy stopped, hands in the air. "These green – " He started walking again.

Davis scrambled to keep pace.

"Listen,' Papy said, "You know the drill. Find out everything you can about this guy. Everyone has a weakness."

"I'll get on it," Davis said. "I'll get back to you this afternoon."

Papy saw a colleague — Representative Carpenter — walking down the hall. He took off after him. Again Davis struggled to keep pace.

"Carpenter!" Papy sucked in a little air as he approached the representative from Tampa.

"Good morning, Papy," Carpenter said.

"What's this new bookies thing?"

Carpenter turned an awkward shade of guilty red. He spoke in a stammering whisper. "Hm? Wh- ? Book- wh- um I'll pay him back. You know I'm good for it!"

"I'm not talking about MY bookies," an exasperated Papy blurted. "But now that you mention it - no. Carpenter! I'm talking about another bill to regulate them."

"Oh!" the color returned to normal in Carpenter's pudgy cheeks. "Of course, of course... What?'

"You don't know what I'm talking about, do you," said Papy, as the realization dawned on him, as it so often does, that he would have to take care of this himself or it would never be taken care of at all. "Meet me in the subcommittee room.'

"Can't," Carpenter said. "The subcommittee's using that room."

"Well move them out."

"But it's - it's the - the subcommittee room. They're the subcommittee."

Papy rubbed his face. "Who the hell is this Matheson anyway?"

"Matheson? Matheson? He's a helluva good guy."

Papy looked Carpenter in the eye. "Carpenter," he said calmly, "have you understood one thing I've said to you?"

"Gotta run, Papy — late for the subcommittee."

"Damn it, Carpenter." But Papy was already looking at the backside of one seriously confused state politician.

He turned to Davis, and said, "Get me an hour with that moron. I have to spell everything out ten times to get him to understand anything."

"Right," Davis said. "I'll try to sit him down with you tomorrow afternoon."

They opened the door to Papy's office, a spacious suite - the kind of office that comes with longevity and power. Papy and Davis entered the office, followed by two men. They all nodded to each other, as if everyone was at home in the office, and all were welcome. The two men moved to a couch, lining a far wall. Other couches, as well as easy chairs and ornate tables decorated the room, giving it the feel of a home entertainment room more than an office. Being in the room, you might think you are at an exclusive cocktail party, especially when Papy opened a bottle of whiskey and poured drinks for himself and Davis.

Papy ignored the two men, and they ignored him, and everyone comfortably went on about their business.

"What else we got?" Papy asked.

"We have a couple problems in Key West," Davis said.

"A COUPLE problems?"

"Martins isn't getting the new rate from Eva."

Papy downed his drink. "Damn it," he said.

"She's still paying the old rate, and Martins is, well, let's say he's – "

"He's sweet on her!" Papy shouted. "She's got her hooks in him."

"He doesn't seem to be pressuring her."

"Tell that broad. No, tell Martins to get over her, and conduct his business like a professional."

Davis nodded. "She does seem to have her hooks in him, yes," he said.

"Dames!" Papy shook his head and poured another drink. "That woman needs to be reminded we LET her stay in business. And Martins needs to remember that she's a tramp and not his girlfriend."

Davis looked at Papy waiting for the next sentence. Nothing came. He shifted his stance and pressed ahead. "So we tell Martins – "

"Tell him to shut her down. Hell, I pay him to make these decisions himself. I got bigger fish to fry."

Two more men casually entered the office, and it took on even more of a cocktail party feel. "Morning Papy," one of them said.

Papy gathered himself together. "Bob, Gerald," he said half-heartedly, as if they had exchanged this greeting a thousand times.

Then Prescott entered. Prescott also seemed at home, going straight for the whiskey, but Papy paid more attention to him than to the others.

"Morning Papy," Prescott said.

"Prescott," Papy said, making it sound like an unfinished sentence.

"Damn." Prescott pressed ahead, either unaware or scared of the serious look Papy was giving him. "You see what happened in that game last night? DiMaggio is, he's, he's something else, I'll tell you that. Best ever; EVER! Bottom of the ninth. Incredible. Hey, Papy, I got a helluva line on the Yankees in the series."

Papy became a symbol of calm authority. He stood facing Prescott. He smiled just slightly, just enough to scare Prescott. Papy slowly put his arm on Prescott's shoulder and in a unique combination of friendliness and command, began walking Prescott away from the others in the room.

"Say, Prescott," Papy said. Anyone who knew Papy knew that when he spoke calmly, like this, like he was your best friend in the world, trouble was not far away. "I wanted to have a little conversation with you about that."

"I have, I have the money. I - I will later today," sputtered Prescott.

Papy smiled and patted him on the cheek. He always preferred not to have the full conversation. He liked it when just the mention of a conversation got his point across. He held his hand on Prescott's cheek for a moment, like a proud father looking at his favorite son. "I knew I could count on you, Prescott."

He took his hand away and turned back to Davis. "Anything else, Davis?" he barked, as Prescott quickly slid out the door and went as far away as he could as fast as he could.

"Yes, actually," Davis said.

"Well?"

Davis put a newspaper, the Miami Herald, in front of Papy. There, in bold type, leading off the top of the front page, was Trumbull's "Dear Cuz" column. "Trumbull's been poking around Key West," Davis said.

Papy was quiet. He didn't stun easily, but this was a stunner. He took the paper from Davis, held it out like it contained some vile poison, then shoved it back into Davis's hand.

He went to the phone on his desk, and grabbed the receiver. His anger made his hand shake enough to send the receiver flying before he could grab onto it. He fumbled angrily with the wires and finally got the receiver to his ear.

"Representative Papy," he said to a Capital building operator's voice. "Get me Martin's at the Key West Police Department."

The wait to connect was too much for him. He paced, holding the receiver to his ear, cursing the very wires he was preparing to talk over. 'Goddamn it, Davis," he shouted.

Davis shifted awkwardly and muttered, "Sorry sir."

"How long have you known about this?"

"Just this morning, sir," Davis said.

Papy was pacing violently now. There was still no one at the other end of the line. He moved too far with the receiver, pulling the phone, papers, his photos, various pens and pencils, whiskey glasses, off his desk onto the floor.

"Goddamn it!" was the predictable response, and Davis jumped into action, trying frantically to restore whatever he could to the desk. Papy moved even further away, dragging phone cords away from Davis and making the mess worse.

Finally Martins was on the other end.

"Martins, what the hell is going on down there?"

Davis scrambled to keep the phone from banging into the desk as Papy spoke.

"...Shut her down! I don't care. Do what you're paid to do!"

Davis continued scrambling to put papers, photos, whiskey glasses, and the phone safely back on the desk while Papy ranted.

"Martins, why the hell are you letting Trumbull poke around?... What does he look like!? He looks like a guy with a chip on his shoulder. He's Stephen Trumbull. What do you mean you don't know what he looks like?"

Davis was gently pushing Papy back toward the desk now, holding the phone in his hands, and trying to direct the mess somewhere back toward a flat surface.

"Martins, handle this! Look, get over the dame. Remind her who wears the pants, and then shut Trumbull up."

Papy tried to punctuate this rant by slamming the phone receiver down, but he couldn't locate the rest of the phone among the papers and pens in Davis's arms, and the whole incident would have been comical, if Papy had any sense of humor at all.

He stood, breathing heavily, angry. He looked at Davis, who finally managed to hang the phone up. Davis looked back at him.

"What?" Papy said.

"You're late for a vote sir."

Papy exhaled.

Meanwhile, 600 miles to the south, the Chief of Police of Key West, Martins, sat at his desk looking at his now silent telephone. He was seething. It was bad enough to get yelled at by a man out of control. It was bad enough to be told that you have to break the trust that makes the community function on a day to day basis. On top of it all, he was not appreciated for the work he does do, for the daily maintenance he performs on behalf of Papy. All he ever does is toe the line, work his tail to the bone, juggle everyone's competing egos day in, day out.

He shoved his foot violently toward his phone, and kicked it off his desk onto the floor.

SHUT DOWN

Trumbull had never been married. He tried to be tolerant. He had known a few marriages that did not totally disgust him. He even considered a few couples to be friends, both of them, the husband and the wife.

The idea of getting married himself, though, disgusted him like nothing else. You might as well have suggested that he slowly crush his head in a vice.

There was only one woman in his past who could have ever tempted him.

Sarah was a prostitute who never charged Trumbull a dime.

He respected her. She was classy. She knew her way around a dangerous situation. She had a way of taking control of situations away from boneheaded men. She always told Trumbull the truth. That was the key. Trumbull lived and breathed for truth in all things; news, politics, sex. They were all equal. All he cared about was that a person never lie to him and he was fine with just about everything beyond that.

It isn't that he had no feelings. He had deep feelings for Sarah. That was part of the problem.

His respect for her, and his relationship with her, meant that he tolerated her flings with men from every corner of the Earth. After a couple years Sarah and Trumbull began sharing his Miami apartment. That was considered scandalous. It just happened one day. Her landlord discovered her business and told her to get out. Trumbull offered to put her up "temporarily," and there they were. She would only do business with guys who took a hotel room. The rest of the time she was slowly becoming a homebody.

Trumbull liked the arrangement. He liked Sarah. He could talk to her about hunting game in Africa. He could talk to her about seeing a man with half his leg shot off in the war, about holding the man's half-shot-off leg in his hand while the medic feebly attempted to re-attach it, the blood dripping sloppy red down Trumbull's arm. She didn't flinch. What was not to like?

Upon reflection he began to see this as his one big weakness.

Matters weren't helped any when Sarah slowed down her 'business' and spent more time at the apartment. After another year, she began saying the crazy words.

"I love you," she would say with a quiet giggle, as if not really paying attention to her own words.

Over time, she would say it more like she meant it. Then Trumbull began falling in love with her. He believed that she loved him, and dropped his guard around her.

That was a mistake.

All these years later, Trumbull would think back on it and hate himself for giving in so easily.

She didn't love him. She never did. What the hell is love anyway, he wondered, some fairy tale invented by poets?

Trumbull brooded over these memories as he sat at The Boat Bar that night sipping his scotch. Next to him two men talked excitedly.

"A hundred on DiMaggio to homer," the first man said.

"A hundred? Are you sure?" asked the second.

"And five hundred on the Yankees to win in five."

"In five? You're sure about this?"

"I only got three tonight, but I'm good for it."

"No, no. I can't front you anymore," the second man said. "Either you got cash or you don't."

"I'm good for it. Come on."

"You got three, I can only put you down for three," the second man said.

"Help me out here."

The second man leaned in and spoke more quietly. "Look, I would love to help you," he said, "but the rules are changing. People are tightening things up."

"The first man squirmed and shifted in his seat. "How long have you known me?" He asked, pleadingly.

"You got three; I can only put you down for three."

Trumbull's attention was wrenched from this conversation when Eva walked up to him and sat on the adjoining stool.

"He's back," she said, "The man of mystery."

Trumbull swallowed a mouthful of mediocre scotch and turned to her. "No mystery about me,' he said.

"The way you sit," Eva mused. "The way you look around the room, the way you listen to every conversation."

Trumbull set his glass on the bar and slowly turned toward her. "You're the one I can't figure," he said.

"How come you haven't placed a bet on anything the whole time you've been here?" Eva asked. "How did you know there were other cheaters at the poker table?"

"Which question do you want me to answer first?"

"Do you gamble or don't you?"

"I have no problem putting money down on the right thing," Trumbull said.

"What's the right thing?" she asked. "What's it going to take?"

"When the right thing comes along, I'll let you know," Trumbull said, absently shaking the last bits of ice in his drink.

A girl came urgently up to Eva. She was young maybe 20 at the oldest, pretty in the way 20-year-old girls can be, before they really know anything about life or about themselves. She was repeating Eva's name like it was an alarm bell.

"What is it?" Eva said.

The girl leaned into Eva's ear and said something Trumbull could not hear. Eva's expression changed. She was angry now.

Eva bolted from her bar stool and left without an explanation. The girl followed her out the door of The Boat Bar. Trumbull, intrigued, downed the last ice cube from his glass and went out after them.

Outside, Eva was already across the street. The girl was half-way across. Trumbull casually crossed the street toward a building.

Three policemen stood outside the door of the building. As the girl passed them, one of them said, "Hi, Jeannie," in a familiar manner.

Trumbull walked past the three policemen, paying them little attention. As he entered the building he heard Eva's voice from down a hallway. "Darrel! Darrel! You bastard! What the hell are you – "

And then the voice of Key West's finest police chief, Martins, came from down the hallway.

"Everybody out! Out! Out! Everybody!"

Trumbull heard the tink tink of a police baton tapping on doors.

As Trumbull rounded a hallway corner, he saw a man come out of a room in his boxers, followed by one of the girls, both of them scrambling to put their clothes back on.

"Johnson, get out of here," Martins boomed. "We're shutting this place down."

"Shutting wha-?" Johnson stuttered, frantically buttoning a white shirt.

Then Martins turned toward all gathered and announced, "Turns out this is a house of ill-repute."

"Ill - re - wha?" Johnson said squirming his face into a model of confusion.

"Prostitution, Officer Johnson," Martins said.

"Prosti - oh!" and the matter at hand dawned on Johnson. Half a second passed as his brain processed the situation, and then he did his best to play along. "Why, I have never been so shocked in all my life!" he said. "Where are my PANTS!?"

"Here they are, Honey," the girl said, handing them to him.

"Thank you Louisa," Johnson said, and he finished dressing quickly.

"This establishment is closed until further notice," Martins announced.

Eva was beyond angry at his point. She was livid. "Darrel, what the hell is this?"

Then Martins took hold of Eva's arm, and pulled her inside the door of a nearby room. "I'm sorry, Eva," he said. "I really am. I had no choice."

"That's it?" Eva said. That's all you can say? 'I'm sorry, Eva?' you told me we could find a way around this."

"Papy's putting the squeeze on me. I don't have any pull here."

"You look like you have plenty of pull."

"Orders, Eva. I'm following orders. Give it a week. Things'll go back to the way they were. You'll get settled." There was a pause that you could chop apart with a kitchen knife. Then Martins made one statement too many. "Maybe I could even make it up you - you know - for old time's sake."

Eva had reached a level of disgust that impressed the on-looking Trumbull; seeing a woman achieve such a disgusted state made him happy.

Eva turned from Martins, walked rapidly to a nearby wall-safe and angrily dialed numbers. She opened the safe and pulled out some cash. Quickly, she counted bills. She thrust several bills in Martin's direction and spat out, "There! There's your money. Happy now?"

"Eva, there's no need to get into a tizzy about this."

"Now get out, all of you," Eva commanded. "Get out of here."

She shoved. She cajoled. She pushed people down the hallway. Trumbull was caught in the log-jam of girls, police, and half-dressed men. Eventually they all spilled out into the street.

"I'm sick of looking at your ugly faces," Eva shouted triumphantly, as she slammed the door behind them all.

WITCH HUNT

P apy stood before the gathered reporters, and cleared his throat. He tapped the microphone. It was set up on the steps of the Capital building, so Papy could look down on everyone while he spelled out his victim-hood.

"I want to say this very clearly and for the record," he said. "The beautiful city of Key West, and my people, the citizens of Monroe County have been maligned, and their reputation dirtied by this man Trumbull, and by The Miami Herald. Now, I hold dear, as we all do, the freedoms we enjoy here in these United States of America, and that includes, of course, freedom of speech. But Mr. Trumbull, and The Miami Herald are on an ill-conceived witch hunt. It is as simple as that.

"Key West is one of the crown jewels of this great state of Florida. It is a beautiful, thriving tourist destination, and I consider it an honor to represent my people, the great citizens who call Key West home. Thank you."

Papy ignored the shouts from the reporters, and lead Davis back inside the building. Inside, they looked at each other. Papy exhaled. "I should never have had to go that far," Papy said.

"No," Davis agreed. "No, it should never have gotten this far.'

WE'RE NOT GOING TO KILL YOU

Outside the whorehouse, the cops snickered among themselves. Martins counted the money, meeting approving looks from the other cops, and laughing back with them.

"Good work, everyone," Martins said.

Some of them shoved each other playfully. Then Johnson, the one who had never been so shocked, asked, sheepishly, "Say, um, if we - if that's over with, do you think- ?"

"Do what you have to do, Johnson," Martins said absently.

Johnson went back to the door, knocked weakly, and pulled it slightly open. "Louisa?" he called. "Louisa, honey?" then he went inside to finish being shocked by the presence of prostitution on the premise.

Trumbull had receded back into the shadows, but remained nearby, watching the policemen. He agreed with Eva. They were disgusting men. They were the worst, he felt, dishonest, senseless, uneducated, lacking any true courage. He was caught up in these thoughts when Martins noticed his presence.

"Hey - hey you," Martins said.

Trumbull managed an unwilling, "Yes?"

"What's your name?"

Trumbull knew now that he would have to talk his way out this, and since he didn't like any of these men, he didn't care if they liked him back. He stepped forward into the streetlight, and said, "My mother used to call me Prince Charming. I think she was being sarcastic."

"Come on, Vacation-from-Atlanta," Martins said, threateningly. "Tell us your name."

Trumbull just stared at Martins, trying to gauge his pain threshhold. He didn't answer.

"I don't think you're from Atlanta at all," Martins went on. "I think you're Trumbull from The Miami goddamn Herald."

One of the other cops stepped in front of Trumbull, making a show of his police issue rifle. "How about it, Mr. Newspaperman?"

Trumbull decided these men didn't deserve conversation with him, and tipped his hat playfully. "Good night, gentlemen," he said, and moved away from the policemen.

The two goons from The Boat Bar emerged, seemingly from nowhere, and stepped in Trumbull's way as he tried to leave. Trumbull knew this was going to be bad, and decided to play things cool.

Martins stepped toward Trumbull. "I didn't say we were through with you," he said.

"I don't much care what you do or don't say." Trumbull said. He thought to himself that there was a right way and a wrong way to get out of this. He didn't like these men, though. In fact he despised everything about them. It's always hard to play things cool when you really despise the people threatening you. He stepped toward the goons, partly to test their resolve, partly to make a point. The goons blocked his way.

Martins stepped between Trumbull and the goons, and spoke quietly to them.

They were getting instructions from Martins, and Trumbull thought they would probably carry out whatever those instructions were.

It was at this point that Trumbull knew he would be hurt tonight. The only questions were; How badly, and would he manage to hurt them back?

The policeman with the rifle bumped up against Trumbull with his rifle barrel. "I'm watching you Trumbull," the man said. "Don't try nothing stupid."

Trumbull looked at the policeman. He looked at the rifle barrel. He pushed the business end of the rifle away, and said, "Careful with that thing. You could hurt yourself."

Martins turned back from the goons, and said, "Good night, Mr. Trumbull." He walked away, followed by the other policemen.

Trumbull was left alone with the two goons. He turned to the goons, and stared them down. The moment lasted long enough for Trumbull to let out a short laugh. He walked toward the goons, pushing past them. They wouldn't let him by. He figured they wouldn't. He just had to test them.

Then they let loose on him. One kneed him in the groin, doubling him over. The other introduced his shoe to Trumbull's temple, sending Trumbull down in a swirling show of sky and pavement.

He lay there for a moment gathering his wits back together.

When he managed to focus his eyes back on the two men standing over him, one of them said, "No need to fight back, Trumbull."

"We don't lose," the other said. And they grabbed his collar and dragged him into the alley. Together the two goons picked him up into a sitting position against the wall of the building.

Trumbull was hurting, but nothing he couldn't suck up.

"Don't worry, Mr. Trumbull. We're not going to kill you," said the first goon.

"We're going to let you live to feel the pain."

Trumbull looked up at the two, feeling nothing but disgust and derision. "You two are a good pair," he said. "I can see how much you both love each other."

The goons didn't seem to appreciate the comment, and within a half-second, a knife blade was inside Trumbull's gut.

Trumbull felt the cold steel in his stomach very clearly. He groaned a groan of true shock.

Then the blade was out, and Trumbull could feel his insides separated.

The goons were gone.

Trumbull knew it was bad. He moved his legs, and made an attempt to stand, but pain shot through his entire body. He dropped back down to a sitting position with a grimace that barely told half of what he was feeling. He put his hand inside his coat. He pulled it out, blood dripping from his palm and fingers.

He leaned his back against the brick wall of the building and tried to gauge the problem. He breathed deeply, as deeply as he could, anyway. It was painful to breathe all the way in.

He focused on the pain, on the feeling he had inside where things are supposed to be attached, and now they weren't. Those assholes knew what they were doing, Trumbull thought to himself. He knew that he would live, that they didn't go for the major arteries or organs, that it was just a matter of getting treated as soon as possible. But he also knew that he would be hurting bad for a long while.

A WALKING MESSAGE

Dear Cuz;

When a sharp blade cuts into you, it is quick, cold. You barely realize what is happening at first. It cuts clean, surgically. The pain almost begins with a question mark.

When a dull blade cuts into you, like the one Papy's goons used on me, it saws into you like a rusty kitchen knife. There is no question what is happening, because the pain is crude and dirty."

Trumbull was groaning and writhing on Eva's bed. She was wrapping a large bandage around his naked torso.

It was the next morning. He didn't remember coming inside, but he remembered the last few minutes before passing out.

"Hold still. You're making it bleed more," Eva said.

"Don't tell me to hold still," he said, nastily.

She wasn't going to complain about his mood. "Lay back," she said.

"Don't - Aaagh!" He dropped his head as she pressed the bandage onto the wound.

"Lie down. Relax. I have to clean the wound."

"Alright, alright," he said. He leaned back, slowly, in fits and starts, stopping with each shot of pain, and moving again when it was tolerable.

Eva dabbed at his wound like a professional. She had seen blood before. She didn't like it, but they both knew Trumbull was in good hands. "You're lucky," she said. "They didn't cut too deep."

"Lucky!?"

"You're alive. That's lucky."

Trumbull looked at her. "They chose to let me live," he said. "They wanted to prove something. They were just making a point - Aaagh!"

"Relax," she said, folding blood-stained bandages. She put the folded bandages in a pile at the foot of the bed.

Trumbull's head was on the pillow now, and he spoke while looking straight overhead at the ceiling. "They figured I'd be a walking message, bandaged up, scared."

"Are you scared?" Eva asked.

"Are you?"

"Yes," she said.

"I can't give in to that," Trumbull said. "If I'm walking, I'm after them."

"You're not walking today," Eva said.

"I'll be up later."

Eva looked down at him and shook her head. "And here I am, bandaging you up," she said. "You keep after them, it's just a matter of time until they come after me the same way."

"So quit helping me," Trumbull said matter-of-factly.

She looked at him. She thought about this for a moment, about kicking him out to let him heal up on his own. Then she reached for a nearby bottle and said, "Don't talk for a minute. This is going to sting."

"What's going to - Aaaaaah!" He writhed in pain as she poured the disinfectant onto the wound. "Damn it, woman!"

"You know I have to do this."

"I've had worse than this, and survived without all this nonsense," he barked, wincing in pain again as he finished the sentence.

"You proud, stubborn man," she said, with a sarcastic smile. "I apologize for trying to keep you alive."

MURPHY

Murphy might have lacked Trumbull's cockiness, but he was a good reporter. He worked hard, and did his job the best he could. He had been around the Herald long enough to know when to speak up, and when to keep quiet.

With Trumbull in Key West, Murphy had proposed to Hills, their editor, that he go after the other part of the story, the boring part, but it was a part they needed. So Murphy found himself in Tallahassee, listening to Representative Matheson, on the House Chamber floor, droning on and on in support of his own bill.

"I was elected to accomplish something during my time here in the Florida House Chamber," he said, from the front of the chamber. Half the House seats were empty. State representatives didn't feel compelled to pay attention to the arguments over bills they were set to vote on. Of those present in the chamber, most were not paying attention. Side conversations went on in all corners of the room. You would think they were discussing matters of importance. More of the conversations, though, were about golf scores than about the issues of the day.

"I campaigned on a promise to clean up illegal gambling," Matheson droned, "and I owe it to my constituents to deliver on that promise."

Murphy sat in the press area with a small notebook and pen. He tuned out Matheson's speech and looked out at the room.

He shared Trumbull's disgust with politicians, with corruption and dishonesty. Maybe he expressed it differently. No one expressed things the way Trumbull did. Murphy's greatest fault, Trumbull had once said to him, was that he played by the rules. Trumbull hated playing by the rules. The rules were established by those with power. Those with power needed the press to keep them honest, to hold them accountable.

Murphy's gaze finally found Papy and Representative Carpenter. They were at the back of the chamber, trying to avoid drawing attention to themselves. They spoke quietly into each other's ears.

Murphy watched the two men talking. He sensed something sinister in the conversation, but with no proof, he had to settle for what he could observe. Then he observed something alarming. Papy and Carpenter shook hands, and Murphy was certain he saw Papy slip something into Carpenter's hand as they shook.

Murphy squinted. He was sure he saw it, but was not sure what they had exchanged. The two men patted each other on the back and parted. Papy turned back toward the open chamber, and Carpenter went out through the grand chamber doors. Murphy jotted a note in his small notebook and stood up.

He left the Press area and went out into the hallway outside the chamber. He found Carpenter walking down the hallway toward the congressional offices.

"Representative Carpenter!" he called out.

Carpenter turned. "Yes?" he said, innocently.

"Pat Murphy, of The Miami Herald," Murphy said. "Alright if I ask a question or two?"

"Of course, of course," Carpenter smiled. "What would you like to know?"

"I was wondering how you plan to vote on Representative Matheson's new bill to regulate bookies."

Carpenter's smile faded ever so slightly. "Well..." he stammered. "Uh, I, uh, have to study the various issues involved, and uh, and get back to you on that."

"I noticed," Murphy continued, "that you and Representative Papy were discussing something during Matheson's speech. Would you care to comment on the nature of your discussion with Mr. Papy?"

Carpenter dropped his last pretense of enjoyment and began looking desperately for an escape. "Well, um,, we were discussing, um – " and when he saw Davis down the hall, Carpenter used that as his excuse, and blurted, "Sorry, gotta run."

"What did Papy shove into your hand?" Murphy yelled after him.

Carpenter could not be accused of running, but he carried his plump body as quickly as he could, down the hall away from Murphy and his questions. Murphy stood alone in the hallway, holding his notebook and pen.

In Miami, Editor Hills was on the phone with Trumbull. "How's it feeling?" Hills asked, a slight note of personal interest creeping into his professional tone. "Uh huh, you're able to get up, move around?"

On the other end of the line, Trumbull explained his physical condition and recovery to Hills.

"How soon can you drive back to Miami?" Hills asked, hopefully.

Trumbull spoke quietly but forcefully. "I need to stay, Hills. I'm not done."

"Trumbull, I admire what you're trying to do here, but I can't —"

"We have to keep the pressure on."

These were the arguments Hills never won with Trumbull. He kept trying, though. "Look, Trumbull, the column was great. It was riveting stuff. My problem is that it was about you nearly dying. I'm not willing to lose you, even if it's in exchange for the best damn column ever. Look, we have Murphy in Tallahassee. You can cover a lot of ground sitting safely at your desk, until your insides are back in one piece."

"I'll see you in a few weeks, Hills."

"Trumbull!"

The line was dead.

Hills hung up the phone and rubbed his face with his hands.

Murphy checked in briefly with the paper, on his way back from Tallahassee, but then he continued on down toward the Keys, to his next source.

He pulled up to the entrance check-point of the Boca Chica Naval Station, and rolled down his window as the guard approached his car.

"Yes?" The guard asked.

"Pat Murphy, Miami Herald. I have an appointment with Admiral Baines."

The guard looked down at a sheet attached to his clip board. "Okay," the guard said, "park in the second lot on the left; Building twelve."

Murphy pulled forward and turned left.

Moments later he was in the Admiral's office, listening to Admiral Baines complain. "I've made several requests to Washington, to the FBI, to come down to Key West, and clean this place up. I'm speaking to deaf ears."

Baines was not a big man, but he carried his rank with pride. The walls of his office were decorated with honors and plaques. Behind him hung an enlarged photo of the Admiral posing with a large fish and President Truman.

"And what," asked Murphy, "is your exact concern regarding Key West?"

The Admiral exhaled. "My men have money two days a month. These are young men, fresh faces. We are supposed to be shaping and training the leaders of tomorrow, but this vice den, Key West –" The admiral shook his head, as if that was the proper way to complete the sentence.

"Is it your opinion, Admiral Baines; that illegal gambling does in fact exist in Key West?"

The Admiral looked at Murphy sideways. "Do I look blind to you?" He asked.

"Hm?"

"Here let me check." The admiral picked up a magazine from the surface of his desk. "Nope," he said. "no, I ain't blind. Of course there's gambling in Key West. Hell, you're a reporter. Why don't you go look around a little."

"Why, in your opinion," Murphy continued, trying his best not to respond to the admiral's sarcasm, "why did the Grand Jury investigation fail to prove the existence of gambling?"

"Who was on the grand jury?"

"Sir?"

The admiral leaned forward. "Go through the names of the grand jury. I guarantee you they're all on Papy's payroll."

Back at The Boat Bar, Trumbull had decided to send his own message back to the goons, and to whomever else was paying attention. He walked in the front door, doing his best to keep his composure.

He walked casually through the room. The slots and the roulette wheel went on about their usual business. The poker table had a couple regulars, who were winning the pants off a couple of newcomers.

Trumbull felt a few more eyes on him than he had felt on previous occasions. People knew who he was now. The story must have gotten around.

His usual bar stool was empty. "Scotch, on the rocks," he told the bartender, as he sat.

He had to sit carefully. Certain movements sent pain through his mid-section. He did his best to keep the pain from showing.

Across the room, Walter was watching Trumbull order. The bartender looked toward Walter also, and Walter nodded back to the bartender.

"Does that guy have to approve everyone's drink?" Trumbull asked, as the scotch came.

"You're a special case," the bartender said.

"I'm flattered."

"We're all supposed to see you and be scared."

"Are you scared?" Trumbull asked, taking a sip from the glass.

"Always."

"How much you lose in kickbacks?" Trumbull asked.

"Can't talk about that," The bartender said.

Trumbull brought the glass back to his lips, but held it under his nose, and took in the smell of the Scotch whiskey. It wasn't great, but it would do. "You can be anonymous," he said.

"You're asking for real information."

"Yeah," Trumbull mused with another sip, "we newspapermen have this funny idea that the public deserves to be informed."

"I'll let you know," the bartender said, as he moved away to serve a customer.

Trumbull sat on his stool and again looked out over the room. How many people does Papy have under his thumb, he wondered. This bartender may be a key part of the story.

THE MAN WITH THE BUCKET OF FISH

The next morning Trumbull stepped outside and felt the sun on his face. It was a beautiful morning in Key West.

He walked around the corner and off of Duval Street. He had begun to notice that the side streets felt different from Duval. The people were less likely to be visitors; the language was Spanish as often as English. The desperation bubbled closer to the surface. The poverty and worry showed on the people's faces.

He noticed once again a group of people gathered around a man with a large bag full of balls. Everyone in the crowd held out their *Bolita* tickets toward the man.

The man, from the middle of the crowd, threw the bag. A lady not far away caught the bag. Everyone was all smiles. This was a part of their day.

The lady reached into the bag with her eyes shut. She pulled out a ball and read the number printed on the ball. A second woman gave out a happy shriek. She was the winner of that day's *Bolita*.

A small-scale celebration sprung up. The others did not seem to mind that they had not won. They celebrated for their friend anyway.

Then....Papy.

He came slowly around the corner, surrounded by desperate people. He worked them like a professional candidate. He hugged the women, he kissed them. He shook hands with the men, his hand on their shoulders, patting their backs.

Then Trumbull realized Papy was giving out twenty dollar bills.

"Here you go," he said, as he handed out the bills. "Thank you. Remember that's from your friend, Representative Papy. There you go. Who loves you? I love you." And the hugging, the kissing, the handshakes, went on and on.

Trumbull watched from across the street. He was smart enough to duck around the corner this time. The scene made him want to throw up.

"And don't forget to vote for your friend again," Papy said, handing out more bills. Two weeks. Do you vote?"

"I no vote," the woman said. "*Cubana* — not citizen."

"Not a problem," Papy said. "Just go to the polling place. Tell them you want to vote for Papy. They'll take care of you." As she nodded back, not entirely sure what he had told her to do, Papy handed her another Twenty.

"*Gracias*," the woman said, holding her hands together in a prayer-like thank you.

"*De nada, de nada*," Papy assured her.

Trumbull turned and walked behind the building back to his hotel, where he would sit down and type out his column. He tried his best to describe what he had seen. It wasn't easy. The scene he had witnessed defied description. His column, which appeared in the next morning's Herald, wrapped up his observation with:

"It was a feeding frenzy. The starving sharks in the tank at the aquarium, swarming around the man with the bucket of fish. Papy had them eating out of his hand."

Back at Boca Chica, Murphy was sitting in the office of the Chaplain. He struck Murphy as a good man. It's an odd thing, being a chaplain to Navy recruits, Murphy thought. The man seemed to genuinely care about the men under his charge, but he could not be naïve enough to think that he meant anything to the men until they were in battle, scared and close to death.

Murphy prompted the Chaplain to explain his misgivings.

"Sometimes, Mr. Murphy," the Chaplain said, "I despair for these boys. Men, we call them men, but they are mere boys, eighteen, nineteen years old."

Murphy shifted in his seat. "Is it your opinion, Chaplain, that the presence of gambling is a poor influence on the men here?"

"My sailors come in, and I hear the same thing over and over again; 'Chaplain, I had a perfect record until I was stationed here at Boca Chica.' I am supposed to minister to men's souls. This vice-center makes my job impossible."

Later that night Eva had suggested that she and Trumbull try a change of scenery. The Boat Bar just didn't seem to have its old magic.

Trumbull reluctantly went along as she introduced him to the wild swinging Cuban music at a smaller bar four blocks away. He didn't really want to be there. It wasn't Eva's fault. The music was lively enough. The patrons: happy, dancing, drinking. Something nagged at Trumbull, though.

He stood near the bar, absently watching the drummer of the Cuban band go at the drums set in a semi-circle around him.

Eva noticed that he was lost in thought. She let it go for a while. Then she decided she hadn't brought him here just to watch him drink and brood.

"What woman was it who hurt you so bad?" She asked.

Trumbull didn't respond at first.

She moved closer to him, trying to get into his line of sight.

"Another drink?" Trumbull asked.

She smiled and swung her hips to the music. "Trumbull," she said, pausing momentarily, "I know I shouldn't say this, but I could get to liking you. I'm not saying I do like you but, let's say, if you ever bothered to act even a little bit like a gentleman."

"Papy's in town," Trumbull said.

"That's it, change the subject."

"He was giving cash to people in the street this morning."

"How do you think he keeps getting re-elected?" Eva asked, annoyed at the turn of the conversation.

"Would you be willing to go on record as a witness to that?" Trumbull asked.

"I was hoping you would leave the reporter at home, tonight. I was hoping I would be more than a source."

Trumbull raised his drink to his lips. He swallowed and shook the ice. He looked at Eva. "Well, are you willing to go on record?"

She rolled her eyes. She had lost this round. "Trumbull, I run a whorehouse. Who do you think is going down when this turns into a battle?"

"There's a weakness here somewhere," Trumbull said. "We just have to find it."

"Let's get out of here," she said.

"I'm not finished with my drink."

"No," Eva said. "No, I guess you aren't." She stood watching his face, trying to read whether he was playing some game with her, or if this was just who he was. "Good night, Trumbull," she said.

"Good night."

She walked out of the bar, swinging her hips to the music again, as she walked. At the door she turned back. He was still looking at nothing, thinking. It's who he is, she thought. That's just who the bastard really is.

THE GOOD STUFF

The Boat Bar was a lot quieter in the early afternoon. A few people pulled the occasional slots. The same bartender cleaned the top of the bar.

The poker table was empty, and the roulette wheel sat idle.

Into this temporary quiet, Papy sauntered through the door like a king entering his castle. He didn't say anything at first, but his presence was felt instantly. The bartender nervously acted busier than he was.

Papy put his hand on Walter's shoulder and spoke quietly. The bartender could not overhear the conversation, but he could tell it was serious. Walter and Papy only said important things to each other. Walter never spoke unless it meant something.

Moments later, while Papy and Walter still stood near the door, still speaking quietly to each other, Police Chief Martins entered.

All three stood in a circle, speaking in hushed tones. Eventually the three men made their way to a table in a secluded corner of the bar.

The bartender tried not to pay attention. It wasn't smart to nose into these conversations. He was suddenly jarred to attention, though, as Papy called to him.

"Three beers." Papy shouted.

The bartender nodded back, pulled three glasses and one by one held them under the tap. He set them on a tray and walked carefully to the secluded corner.

"Thank you," Papy said, as he tapped the bartender on the shoulder with a smile.

After returning to the bar, he turned back, and saw Martins pulling out a large envelope filled with money. It was a lot of money. The three men began separating the money on the table top and began counting it, careful not to let their beer glasses get the bills wet.

The bartender fought his urge to gawk. Best to play dumb, he thought, so he busied himself with useless tasks, and nervously dragged the bar towel across the bar again and again.

The next twenty minutes passed slowly for the bartender. A scrawny-looking man who had spent an hour or so losing his precious coins into a slot machine stopped at the bar for a beer.

"Helluva thing," the scrawny man said. "I can have good luck four days in a row, and then nothing for months. I don't get it."

The bartender leaned his elbows on the bar and absently said, "Trick is to sit tight until those four days are gonna come around again."

"The hell you say. The hell you say."

When the scrawny man left, the bartender tried not to be too obvious, but he found himself perking an ear up toward the secluded corner. Something was not right there. Papy was agitated, and Martins was talking fast.

Walter sat in his chair passively, as he always sat. But Papy and Martins were going at each other about something.

The bartender wasn't sure whether to be scared or fascinated. Then he distinctly heard Papy say, "This stops now! Do you hear me? This is no longer being discussed."

The bartender raised his eyebrows at this, but had to tend to business, as Trumbull sat down. The bartender had not seen him come in.

"The usual," Trumbull said.

The bartender got the usual: glass, ice, scotch.

"You get a good night's sleep?" Trumbull asked him.

"Sure."

"You do any thinking about what we talked about?"

The bartender quietly panicked, and nervously glanced toward the secluded corner. This was not a conversation he wanted right now. "Don't know what you're talking about," he said.

Trumbull knew he was nervous, but he would never let that stop him from pressing ahead. "I'm talking about protecting you as an anonymous source," Trumbull said. "Give me a little insight into the lowlifes sitting over at that table."

The bartender nervously wiped his towel across the bar. "Like I said, I don't know what you're talking about."

At this point Papy and Trumbull made eye contact. Papy rose from his chair. He sauntered over to Trumbull slowly, enjoying the moment, enjoying it a little too much, Trumbull thought. Papy had a way of walking that said, I'm going to defeat you and you'll be my goddamn friend afterwards. Trumbull felt the hostility rising in him.

"Mr. Trumbull, it is so good to see you up and active," Papy said. "I was sorry to hear about your accident."

"Yes, I'm sure you were all broken up about it," Trumbull said dryly.

"Won't you come join us?" Papy said. "I don't think you've been properly introduced to my friends. What are you drinking?"

"The cheap swill you let your bartender pass off as scotch."

Papy smiled and turned to the bartender. "The good stuff," he said.

The bartender nodded and turned away. He pulled a bottle off the highest shelf and grabbed a clean glass. He turned to Trumbull and poured generously. He slid the glass in front of Trumbull.

Trumbull held the glass. He did not drink right away. He let the aroma of the scotch percolate under his nose. He took a sip. He smiled one of his rare smiles. "You amaze me, Papy," he said.

"Come join us"

Papy turned and began his confident saunter back to the secluded corner. Trumbull stayed seated for a moment. He considered drawing the line here, before Papy could turn his charm any higher, and cloud his judgment. Finally Trumbull stood and followed.

"Chief Martins, let me introduce Mr. Trumbull, of the Miami Herald, a legendary writer and columnist." Papy was indeed turning the charm up high.

"We've met," Martins said.

"Yes," said Trumbull, "Martins and I seem to have a hard time avoiding each other."

"Well, great," Papy said, "to friends, then. We are all friends at this table."

Martins looked out of the corner of his eye. "We could think of this as a new beginning," he said sarcastically.

Trumbull felt one of those dark moments, when he knew he was about to say something unsafe. "I can only hope you'll be as good a friend to me as you are to Eva."

Martins looked at Trumbull directly now. "What exactly do you mean by that, Mr. Trumbull?"

"Gentlemen, gentlemen," Papy said, calmly. "Come now, let's put hard feelings aside. I'm sure Mr. Trumbull is a reasonable man. Hm, Mr. Trumbull? You're a reasonable man, aren't you?"

"Your definition of 'reasonable' or mine?" Trumbull asked.

Papy knew when charm wasn't working, so he changed tone. "We offer you hospitality, friendship. You respond with innuendo. Come now, Mr. Trumbull. This could all work out very well for all of us."

Papy and Trumbull eyed each other.

"There are ways we can make this satisfactory for all involved," Papy went on. He sat so that Trumbull could very clearly see the cash they had been counting, as it poked out of his inside jacket pocket. "Mr. Trumbull, there is no call for finger pointing, name calling. Just say what you want. Let me know what would be satisfactory for you. I'm sure we can come to an agreement."

Trumbull held himself back from lunging across the table at Papy. He calmly took a breath.

Papy was always uncomfortable with long silences. "We wouldn't want a repeat of the unfortunate circumstances that caused you so much pain recently," he said.

"Cut the bullshit, Papy." Trumbull had held himself back as long as he could. "You want to soften me up, impress me with good scotch, treat me like these idiots who do your dirty work. You thought I'd be scared after your goons sliced me open. You can go to hell, Papy. And I'm gonna help you get there."

Both men were standing now. "Leave us to run our town the way we see fit, Trumbull."

"Sure, get out of the way. Hear no evil, see no evil, like goddamn monkeys."

"You're not as big a deal as you think, Trumbull." Papy was speaking forcefully, angrily. He spoke like a man who had power and knew it. "You're just a mosquito, flying around my face. Well you know what happens, right. You fly too close and the next thing you know I swat you. You're nothing, a dead mosquito."

"You make me laugh," Trumbull said, matching Papy's tone. "You think you can scare me with a couple of Cuban goons. They made a big, big mistake, Papy. They let me live."

The two men were in each other's faces now, hands approaching each other's necks. Walter and Martins were trying to step between the two men.

"Don't make the mistake of touching me," Papy warned.

"This is for Bill Lee," Trumbull barked. "Remember him? Good man, poking around after the truth. Thought you could silence him"

Papy pushed Trumbull's shoulder back a few inches, and within a split second the tussle escalated to near fistfighting. Neither man landed a solid blow, partly due to the interference of Walter and Martins.

Martins grabbed Trumbull's arms from behind and pulled him back, shouting, "Hey now! Hey, this is Key West."

Trumbull, despite all of his pride and confidence, felt his wound open, and the pain shot through him like a lightening bolt. He doubled over and groaned. Down on a knee, he breathed and held his stomach.

Papy shook Walter's hands off his own shoulders and adjusted his jacket. "Trumbull, you better watch yourself," he said. "You're in no condition for this fight."

Trumbull gathered his breath and looked up. "Think you can take me on, Papy? You have no idea."

Papy laughed. "You're the one who has no idea," he said, and gathered his things together from the table and walked out.

Ask a Man What He's Angry About

Eva once again stood over Trumbull, looking down at his wound. He was on her bed, shirt off, bleeding on her beautiful white sheets. She had put him there, after he stumbled in from outside. She stared at him. Her mood was a mix of compassion and disbelief. She shook her head and furrowed her eye brows. Then she began to smile. It was not a smile of happiness. It was a smile of cynicism.

For his part, Trumbull did his best to breath calmly and let the wound re-heal. He needed a little help, though. Finally he lifted his head toward Eva. "You gonna do something or stand there and wait for me to die?"

"I don't know why I do it," she said. "What do I get out of this? I nurse you back to health. I'm going to be shut down for good after this one."

"If you're not going to bandage me up, just say so, and I'll drive myself to the hospital."

"You should," she said. "You need a hospital. You're too much for me."

Trumbull made an attempt to sit up. He moved with grunts and an occasional gasp as the pain moved through him. Then the blood dripped on the sheet some more and Eva put her hand to his shoulder.

"Lie back down," she said.

Trumbull didn't respond right away. His intention was to continue getting up, but the pain won the argument for him, and he dropped back onto the pillow.

She dabbed at his red-stained torso. She worked in silence for several minutes, again pouring the disinfectant onto the wound. Trumbull was prepared this time, and did not make a sound. She could feel his body tense up, though.

As the sting subsided, Trumbull let out a slow exhale. Eva grabbed several towels and cleaned him up. "You stupid, stupid man," she said.

Trumbull managed a quiet laugh, and muttered, "You have such a refreshing bedside manner."

She wrapped the fresh bandages around him, and pinned them into place.

"What drives you, Stephen?" she asked.

"Don't ever call me Stephen....ever," he said quietly.

Why not?"

"... ever."

She continued looking down at him. Her curiosity was raised.

She smirked and picked up the used towels and bandages. She busied herself for several minutes, cleaning up and arranging medical supplies. She felt like kicking him out.

She decided not to.

At The Boat Bar, Papy stood with his arm around the bartender's shoulder. The regulars were there. That is to say, the regulars of these sorts of scenes: Walter, Martins, the goons.

Papy was utilizing his favorite friend-of-the-family stance, smiling, patting the bartender on the shoulder. The bartender's protests, though, had the sound of worry in them.

"No," the bartender said, "I haven't talked to him."

Papy spoke calmly, soothingly. "You know, being a bartender puts you in a very unique position. People come in here, they have a few drinks; lips begin to loosen up."

"I haven't talked to him,"

"Has he asked you anything? "Papy said.

"He tried. He asked if I wanted to be anonymous. I said no. I didn't talk to him."

Papy took his arm off the bartender's shoulder. He moved a few feet away, making eye contact with one of the goons.

Nothing was said, but the goon knew his job. He walked up to the bartender, and smiled at him.

Papy's tone was different as he turned and spoke to the bartender. "Do you like living in Key West?"

"Yes, of course."

"It's a beautiful town," Papy said.

"Yes, yes of course it is."

"Lovely people, good friends," Papy said.

"Uh huh, yes."

"You wouldn't want to jeopardize the nice life you have here," Papy said.

"Of course not."

Papy nodded to the goon, who took hold of the bartender's right hand. The goon's grip was tight. He pulled three fingers straight and put the three fingers on the edge of the bar. He held the fingers there. The bartender's breathing increased rapidly, and his eyes opened wide.

Papy continued, "Do you know what happens to people who jeopardize their beautiful life here in Key West?"

"I swear I didn't say anything to him."

Papy motioned to the goon to let the hand free. The goon released his grip and the bartender pulled his hand away quickly, feeling it with the fingers of his left hand, holding them close to his chest.

"I believe you," Papy said.

Papy moved close to the bartender, and again adopted a friendly, fatherly tone. "I'm not going to hurt you. No, not a good chap like you." He patted the bartenders face. "I'm not going to hurt you. In fact –" Papy pulled a twenty dollar bill out of his pocket. "I'm going to reward you for your well done work."

He put the twenty directly into the bartender's shirt pocket, punctuating the move with a friendly pat to the front of the pocket. "Remember who loves you," Papy said.

With one last friendly pat to the bartender's cheek, Papy turned away and gathered his coat. As he walked out of the bar, the others slowly dispersed; Walter to his regular chair on the far side of the room, the goons out the back door. Martins followed Papy out the front.

As they left him, the bartender breathed a sigh of genuine relief. He felt the Twenty in his pocket, and looked down, unsure whether to be happy he was alive, or disappointed that he had once again been bought off by Papy.

In Eva's room, Trumbull ate hungrily from a soup bowl. He was still on her bed, legs stretched out straight in front of him. He leaned over the bowl with each spoonful.

Eva stood at the end of the bed. Finally she spoke. "You going to tell me?" she asked.

"I don't really want to talk about it," Trumbull said, dipping the spoon in the soup again and bending down as he slurped.

She pulled a chair up next to the bed. "You will, though," she said.

She sat and watched him eat. The soup bowl was nearly empty now. He brought the bowl up to his mouth and scooped the last of the soup into his mouth with the spoon. As he tilted the empty bowl away, she reached for it. She got up and took the bowl away. When she came back, she sat back in the chair and faced him without saying anything.

She looked at him expectantly.

He avoided her gaze for a minute, thinking. Then he relented. "My father was in politics," Trumbull said.

"It's a funny thing," Eva aid. "Whenever you ask a man what he's angry about, the story always begins, 'My father-.' My father did this, my father did that."

"I'll let you finish the story, you know so much," Trumbull muttered quietly.

"Sorry, I'm listening."

Trumbull took a moment. He was not accustomed to telling this story. Most of his life was spent brooding over the things he was about to tell Eva. But he preferred to keep them to himself.

"He was the most hypocritical man I ever knew." He stopped and looked at Eva. He would continue only if he was sure she would really listen. He continued, "I believed every word he said, for so many years, and then –" he trailed off.

"Then you discovered the lie," she said.

"I was thirteen years old. I idolized him up to that point."

Eva let out a quiet sigh. "I learned at a very young age, never to idolize a man," she said

Trumbull adjusted his position, grunting slightly at a light shot of pain as he moved. "It was like a punch in the gut," he said. "knocked the wind right out of me, like I literally couldn't breathe. I overheard him in the kitchen of our house."

He stopped again, looking down at nothing. Eva kept quiet.

Then he said, "He accepted money from some two-bit –"

"They bought his vote," she said.

He looked at her. "Everything I thought I knew about him came crashing down; principals, beliefs, what's right, what's wrong."

Trumbull's personal guard was down in that moment. She gave him a look of support. He dropped his gaze again, and adjusted the bed sheet.

A FLORIDA STORY

Editor Hills sat at the end of the Miami Herald's large conference room table with his feet up on the edge of the table. He looked casual, but he was serious. Big decisions were made every day in this room. He made these decisions, and the fact that he did it every day, allowed him some freedom to put his feet up when he made them. He held a piece of paper in front of him.

Murphy was at the chair around the corner of the table. Two other senior Editors sat across from Murphy, and two more reporters sat further down the table. They all watched Hills as he read.

Hills took his red pen from his shirt pocket and ran a line through something he read. One of the senior editors looked down and shifted in his chair.

Finally Hills looked up. "Okay," he said, "What are we leading with?"

"With that," the Senior Editor said.

Hills looked back down at the paper in his hand. "Pyongyang talks in Korea are important," He said, "but does it lead?"

"Pretty important story, I'd say," the other Editor said.

Hills put the piece of paper on the table and reached for a small stack in front of Murphy. "I like Murphy's Boca Chica story," he said.

"I hear you're getting some heat from all this Papy stuff," the other Editor said.

"Yeah, we're getting heat, alright," Hills said. "I am aware of it, maybe more so even than you are. That's why I made Murphy rewrite this several times. We have to be very careful how we proceed."

"I was having a couple drinks with Pendergrass, from the Times."

"Consorting with the enemy," Hills said, chuckling.

"Watch out, now," said one of the reporters at the end of the table, "we'll be accused of colluding on the news coverage."

Laughter scattered around the room, until the other editor finally finished his thought, "He asked why we're so intent on bringing Papy down. Who cares what goes on in Key West?"

Hills took his feet down and returned them to the floor. He scooted forward and set the papers on the table. "Here are some things we know, that we can't write on the front page of a newspaper, because it is opinion; one, Florida has very little true leadership in the Statehouse. Two, what passes for leadership is guys like Papy running little fiefdoms around the state."

"We do run that on the front page," the other editor said. "We do it under Trumbull's 'Dear Cuz' column."

"Yes, we do," Hills said. "Trumbull has earned himself the freedom to go public in that way, but that's different from you and me and Murphy, under the guise of hard news reporting, exposing facts that are backed up with hard evidence and hard sources. Murphy's story from Boca Chica begins to crack that nut."

"We're putting the reputation of the Herald on the line, the longer we go with this."

"We certainly are doing that," Hills said. "We're putting our reputation on the chopping block if we pass on it, too. Now with Murphy's story we do not mention Papy."

Murphy jumped into the fray at this point. "We're separating the two things," he said.

"What two things?" asked the other editor.

"Gambling in Key West," Murphy said. "It's a separate story from Papy himself."

Hills moved the papers into separate stacks in front of him and added, "Papy's corrupt control of Key West has to wait, for now. We're just exposing the existence of illegal gambling."

"What's Trumbull's column?"

Hills looked at Murphy. "Trumbull is sending his column in late. We haven't seen it yet."

There were looks around the room. The other Editor coughed. "Hills you better be careful, running Trumbull late, without a thorough check."

"Are you telling me how to do my job?" Hills asked

"Just being a voice of reason."

"Alright," Hills said. "You've had your say. You're the voice of reason. Let's move on."

"Are we really leading with this, and burying the Korean war?"

"Someone wins the war, we'll lead with that," Hills said, his patience running short. "We're a Florida paper. We're leading with a Florida story. Now what else do we have?"

One of the reporters at the other end of the table said, "There're also the murders in South Beach."

"Yes," Hills said, calming slightly. "Good story. Nice reporting. Teaser at the bottom of page one. Put the rest inside somewhere. Alright gentlemen, good work. Let's get out there and find news that doesn't want to be found."

INTIMIDATION AND BENEVOLENCE

Dear Cuz;

There's an old story about Al Capone; that he ran Chicago so completely, so absolutely, that the Mayor called him up one day and said, "Hey Al, The President is coming to town. Do you think we could keep things under wraps while the President is in town? You know, crime, murder: the obvious things. It would look bad to have some big headline while the President is here."

Terms were discussed, an agreement reached, and crime in Chicago was pretty much non-existent for a week. The Mayor was seen later that month, attending Capone's birthday celebration. The two loved each other. The Mayor never referred to Capone as anything but a Brother and benefactor to all good things about Chicago.

Capone was funny that way. The people who loved him, loved him so thoroughly that they would bend over backwards to sing his praises. I think if you looked closely, though, if you knew what to look for, you would see the fear hidden deep in their eyes.

There are two big differences between Al Capone and Bernie Papy.

The first difference is that Papy isn't just partners with an elected official. He is an elected official. He is THE elected official, for Monroe County anyway.

The second difference is that, compared to Chicago, Papy's fiefdom of Key West is amateur-hour.

He utilizes the same tactics, though. He runs Key West to the benefit of a few, himself and his close group of pathetic cronies. He keeps the citizenry in line through a mix of intimidation and benevolence. One day he will pat you on the face, smile at you, and hand you money. The next day he will leave you to rot in a dark alley, or break a finger or two, to remind you who calls the shots.

Papy refers to the citizens of Key West as "My people." He says it a lot, "My people want this; my people want that." He wants you to think he says it as a friend, like his people are family; that he cares about them like no one else does.

Don't kid yourself. When Papy refers to "My people," he is doing it because he thinks he owns them.

Last night I awoke in the middle of the night to a gun shot in the alley behind my hotel. I'm sure I was not the only person who heard it. I was the only person who was curious, though. When I dressed and went downstairs and outside, not a soul was stirring. Especially not the poor stiff in the alley who had crossed Papy's wishes. He was left bleeding into a gutter, like Bill Lee was a year ago after he ran his piece in the local paper.

A few nights earlier I heard a scream from a few blocks away. Maybe they just broke something, the man's hand, or his leg. Or maybe they did to him what they did to me.

I will continue to write about Papy, and his amateur-hour fiefdom, because Papy thinks I will stop at some point.

I will not stop.

-Trumbull

IT'S EMPTY

Trumbull had often marveled at the roosters wandering the streets, their combs and wattles and saddle feathers cut off by their handlers, to give them an edge against the other roosters.

The cock-fighting pit was away from downtown Key West, but not so far away that you wouldn't notice when the fights were going on.

Trumbull stopped on his way to The Boat Bar, hearing the cheering from the cock-fighting pit. He walked the several blocks to the pit, and saw the men gathered around, cheering for their birds.

By the time he reached the edge of the crowd, the fight was over, won by the favorite, a black bird with muscular legs. As the crowd slowly dispersed, one man was having a hard time coming to grips with the fact that he had bet on the wrong bird. Trumbull waited to see who the somewhat familiar voice was, and when enough of the men had walked away and cleared his view, he saw Prescott gesturing angrily.

Trumbull was familiar with Prescott by now, and always expected that someday Prescott would lose his mind. This appeared to be the moment, as Prescott drew a small pistol from his belt, aimed it at the victorious rooster, and pulled the trigger. The rooster blew apart in an explosion of feathers.

A silent moment passed.

Then several of the men attacked Prescott, wrestling the gun out of his hands, and shoving him to the ground.

Trumbull smirked at this comical sequence of events and turned to leave.

He walked into The Boat Bar, which was in the middle of a quiet afternoon, and walked up to the bar. He sat, turned to the bartender, and said, "The good stuff."

The bartender wiped his towel across the bar where Trumbull elbow was. "We're out," he said. "You can have the usual."

Trumbull looked up at the top shelf behind the bar. "Is that right?"

"Yes, we're out."

"Funny," Trumbull said, dryly, "I can see the bottle."

"It's empty."

"Is that how it is?" Trumbull asked, nodding his understanding of the bartender's situation.

The bartender poured a beer for another customer, and walked back to Trumbull. "Do you want the drink or not? It don't matter to me either way."

"I'll have the drink," Trumbull said.

The bartender turned and grabbed the glass, bottle, and ice, and poured Trumbull's drink. Trumbull took it, drank some, and turned out to survey the mostly empty room.

"I know you're scared," Trumbull said. "I would never use your name. In fact I'll make up a fake name. I'll use as my source, Larry Smith, boat-worker at the docks."

The bartender mechanically put away clean glasses, avoiding eye-contact with Trumbull. Finally he said, matter-of-factly, "I don't know anything. I don't want to talk to you."

MAY HE ALWAYS LAND ON HIS ASS

Papy's office was loud and noisy, even more so than usual. It was a happy sort of noisy, raucous even.

Murphy hung back, down the hall, checking the doorways and nooks for the best place to eves-drop.

Inside the office, Papy was pouring drinks for Carpenter and several of their colleagues. "A Toast!" Papy said, raising his glass. "A toast to Representative Matheson of Palm Beach!"

"Here! Here! To Matheson!" Carpenter repeated.

"May he learn his lesson, and get voted out," Papy continued. "Oh, by the way, Davis, who do we have in Palm Beach? Who can we run against him?"

Davis downed a swig of his drink and coughed. "I'll look into it," he said with a smile.

Papy raised his glass again, "To the death of his ridiculous attempts to regulate bookies."

"Here! here!" cheered Carpenter.

Glasses clinked together and were tipped back. The alcohol flowed easily for Four O'clock in the afternoon.

Down the hall, Murphy had found a good spot. He sat on a marble ledge, around the corner from the hallway to Papy's office, but with Papy's door open, he could easily overhear everything being said. He marveled at the open laughter and derision with which the elected officials spoke of Matheson. There was so much laughter coming from the room, Murphy could only guess at the number of men inside.

The true number was an even dozen, and more were on their way.

Papy interrupted a round of laughter. "Say, did I tell you about Traynor, from Jacksonville?"

"Traynor... Traynor," Carpenter mused.

"Looks like a damn Sunday school teacher. Always wears a bow tie."

"Oh, Traynor, yes."

"So I comes up to him," Papy began, just as he was interrupted by the arrival of two more elected officials.

"I heard there's a celebration going on in here," one of the newcomers shouted.

"Gentlemen," Papy said warmly. "Come have a drink. Davis, pour these men whatever they want."

The newcomer gladly accepted the glass from Davis and said, "If I didn't know better I'd think you ran the House Bar, not one of the key political offices in Florida."

"The two things can be one and the same, Jeffrey," Papy said, putting his arm around the man's shoulder.

"To Papy!" the newcomer said, raising his glass

"Here here," Carpenter again shouted.

The newcomer looked at Carpenter, smiled a pained smile, and continued, "May Papy live a long and prosperous life, and kill more pointless legislation!"

"Wait, wait," Papy said, "I was about to tell that story about Traynor."

"Traynor, Traynor, oh, yes, the Sunday School Teacher?"

"You know the one," Papy said.

"Let's hear it," said the newcomer.

"Okay." Papy set his glass down, and cleared his throat. The room quieted down in anticipation. "So, I goes up to him in the hallway. He's deep in thought, probably wondering whether to introduce legislation to make the milk the state drink." A rumble of laughter rolled through the office. "I comes up behind him, and puts my hand on his shoulder, right? First, he nearly jumps out of his skin. Then I calms him down. I ask him, 'Reprehoo Traynor,' I says, 'I want to discuss this bill of Matheson's with you.' I shake his hand, right? And I has a bill in my palm, of course. He looks at the bill, looks at me like I'm the Devil hisself. He drops the bill, and runs away, and, get this, he runs smack into the door of the ladies restroom, as someone is coming out. Knocks him clean on his ass."

The laughter was accompanied by clapping and assorted hoots.

The newcomer raised his glass again and shouted, "To Traynor!"

"Here here," said Carpenter.

"May he always land on his ass!" Papy said.

Glasses clinked together and alcohol flowed down the throats of Florida's best and brightest.

Murphy was writing in his notebook as he jogged down the hallway to leave the building. He nearly ran into a woman who was entering as he tried to exit. He apologized and continued down the steps toward the parking lot.

At his car he did not get in right away. He stood beside the car, and rested the notebook on the roof, writing furiously, flipping the small pages as he scribbled his notes. Finally he folded the notebook and put it in his coat pocket, opened the car door and started the car.

IT'S A STORY, NOT A STORY

Hills was on his way out of his office, when Murphy, who had just made it back to Miami a half-hour earlier, pulled his completed story out of his typewriter. He saw Hills making his exit through the newsroom, and ran up to him with the copy. Hills looked at the papers in Murphy's hands, and leaned back onto a nearby desk.

The two sat quietly while Hills read the new story.

He flipped one page over, read some more, flipped another page over. Murphy was patient but nervous.

Finally Hills looked up from the papers and handed them back to Murphy. He didn't say anything right away. This made Murphy even more nervous.

"He's buying votes," Murphy said.

Hills tapped the desk a few times, and said, "He might be buying votes, but you don't have it here."

"It's his own words."

"It's a story about a guy telling a story," Hills said. "You overheard a guy, drinking, telling a story. I'm sorry, it's not evidence."

"Come on, Hills, you've been listening too much to these guys hanging out with the Times writers?"

Hills stood and looked intently at Murphy. "You're a good reporter, Murphy. I go to bat for you as long as you do your best work. This is not your best work. It's a story, not a STORY. You get the difference? Don't start pulling your imitation of Trumbull standing up to me. Trumbull and I have a deep understanding and it starts with getting the writing done right."

"I'm sorry, Hills," Murphy said with his head down. "Sorry, I guess we're all working a little harder than usual on this one. Maybe it's getting to me."

"Don't let it get to you yet, Murphy," Hills said. "You're just getting started on this."

"Alright, I get it. It's a man telling a story, but the story he's telling is true."

"So you back it up," Hills said. "We can't go to print with an overheard conversation of people drinking. Maybe the fact that they were all drinking in the afternoon would raise some eyebrows, but nobody would care for more than twenty minutes. You back this information up. You get other people. Where's your other source? Where's your interview with this guy Traynor?"

"He didn't return my call. I couldn't find him."

"Well, find him."

Murphy sighed and turned his head away. An Assistant Editor approached to see what the two were talking about.

Murphy looked back toward Hills and said, "It still runs, though, right?"

"What runs?" the Assistant Editor asked.

Hills looked back at the stack of papers, and said, "It's like reporting what guys are telling each other at a bar."

The Assistant Editor took the papers and began looking through them.

Murphy tried one more time, "It's a State Representative telling someone he bought a vote. How is that not a story?"

Hills took a step as if to leave, stopped and turned back. "If Papy holds another press conference accusing us of a witch hunt, and this is what he throws at us, it doesn't stand up. Is it something? Yes, Murphy, okay it's something. It's not what we need, though, until you get more sources. - Someone else accusing Papy of buying votes, that's a story. Papy drinking saying he tried to buy a vote, that's just a story about Papy drinking."

The Assistant Editor held up the papers. "What do you want with this then? " he asked.

Hills turned from Murphy to the Assistant Editor and back. He thought quietly for a moment and said, "Put it on page 12."

Then Hills buttoned his coat and walked the rest of the way through the newsroom and out the door.

The Assistant Editor shifted the papers in his hand, and looked at Murphy. "Well," he said, "it is something." Then he turned and walked away, leaving Murphy alone in the large empty newsroom.

There was a new kind of silence to the newsroom now that Murphy had not felt before.

OF COURSE YOU'RE RIGHT

Police Chief Martins looked up from the report he was filing when the phone on his desk rang. He looked at the receiver. It rang a second time. Somehow he knew it was Papy, and he didn't want to answer it. On the third ring he gave in and picked up the receiver.

"Hello," he said. He was right. It was Papy. And Papy was talking a mile a minute.

"Papy — slow down for a minute." He listened but he was beginning to think of Papy as a crazy man. When did it happen he wondered? It wasn't too long ago that he was all the way on board with Papy. It was profitable for everyone. Things were set up right. Everyone was making money. Then Papy got greedy, stopped listening to reason. Now he was babbling on and on about....what?

"Papy, you can't be serious...no, no, of course you're right...I said you're right!... You're always right. I just ...I have other ways to influence Eva. I don't think we need to go there...Because it's too much. It's not necessary."

At this the babbling, the craziness, the yelling from the other end of the line increased in intensity. Martins pulled the receiver away from his ear. He could still hear Papy's voice loud and clear. He dropped his head to the side and waited for the yelling from the receiver to quiet down.

Finally he brought the receiver back to his ear. "No, I understand," he said. "I understand...of course...yes, yes...you're right, of course you are...alright...goodbye."

Martins slowly returned the receiver to its hook. He took his hand away from the phone and sat back. He exhaled. Then he put his foot on his desk near the phone, and in an angry instant kicked the phone off his desk onto the floor.

I MIGHT BE A DEAD WOMAN

Eva was again swaying her hips to the Latino music that was blasting from the front of the room. Trumbull seemed less moody tonight. He was watching the drummer pound away, in unique rhythms, behind the band. In front of them, the regulars were dancing with abandon.

These people have almost nothing, Trumbull thought, and yet they seem to love being alive so much.

He tipped his drink back and watched Eva's hips swaying.

She turned and smiled at him.

He emptied his drink and said, "Let's go."

They made their way through the dancing crowd, and to the door. Outside, as the door shut, the music quieted to a muffled background sound.

Eva was drunk. Trumbull was too, but he never showed it. She laughed as they stepped out into the street, barely avoiding a honking car.

"What's '*bolita*'?" Trumbull asked.

"What's 'bullshit'?" she responded, swaying unintentionally in the middle of the street.

"*Bolita*, the game the Cubans play."

"Oh." Eva giggled for no reason. "It's a numbers game."

"I figured that much out," Trumbull said.

"The tickets they buy, they have a number on them. Every day they gather together, and they, um, they, they throw the thing, you know."

"Jesus," Trumbull said, cracking the faintest hint of a smile, "learn to hold your alcohol a little bit."

"Sorry we can't all be like the great Stephen Trunkle," Eva said, giggling uncontrollably now.

"Did you just call me 'Trunkle'?"

"That's your name, isn't it?"

Trumbull took her by the arm, and led her across the street. "Now is when you should just stop talking," he said.

As they entered Eva's room, she sat on the bed and bounced up and down on the mattress playfully. Trumbull took his hat off and hung it on the corner of a mirror. He removed his coat and dropped it on a chair. When he turned to Eva, she had begun bouncing more slowly, looking down. Then she stopped bouncing completely, and became serious.

"I think I might be a dead woman, Stephen," she said.

"I told you, don't call me Stephen."

"I might be a dead woman."

Trumbull stood near the chair, and looked at her thoughtfully. "Why?"

She didn't respond at first. She didn't want to say it, or maybe she just wanted to appear reluctant. She looked up at him and said, "Because I think I'm falling in love with you."

Trumbull didn't blink. "No you're not," he said. "I don't buy it. What's your angle here?"

"I have news for you," she said. "Not everyone has an angle."

"Plus, you're not dead. They won't come after you. They won't shut down a place like this. As long as you keep the kickbacks coming, as long as you continue to provide 'services,' they'll leave you alone."

"Fuck the kickbacks," she said defiantly. She stood, moving toward him, angry. "Fuck the kickbacks!" She wavered a little, and he remembered that she was still very drunk.

"Easy now," Trumbull said, holding her steady.

"No more goddamn kickbacks!" she said. "I ain't paying those assholes nothing no more."

Trumbull was holding her more completely now, and she slowly began to give in to his embrace.

"I'd speak a little quieter if I was you," Trumbull said.

"Stephen" she said, looking into his eyes, "you're holding me."

"You're drunk," he said.

"Aren't you going to yell at me for calling you 'Stephen'?"

Holding her with his left arm, he brought his right hand up to her face. He brushed her hair away from her eyes, and ran his thumb along her cheek. Slowly, he brought his lips toward hers and gave her a light kiss.

"Don't ever call me Stephen," he said.

He kissed her again. She returned the kiss, making it more forceful.

"Who called you 'Stephen'?" she asked. "Why do you hate it so much?"

He kissed her again, and they kept the kiss going for a longer period of time. When he pulled away, they both breathed heavily.

"My name's Trumbull," he said. "End of story."

She raised her free arm up over his neck and pulled him close once again.

Early the next morning, Trumbull woke with the sun shining in through the window. He looked over at the sleeping Eva. She was naked, half covered by the bed sheet. He looked at her back, and thought about how much he liked her skin. He sat up half-way against the pillow and looked out the window.

The morning seemed perfect — too perfect, in fact.

As he looked out the window, listening to the chirping of the birds, another sound began to creep into his consciousness. It was low and quiet, almost a rumbling sound. Then he concentrated on the sound, and he didn't like what he heard.

Then he saw the flicker of a flame through the crack of the doorway. Smoke was beginning to flow in under the door.

"Eva!" he shouted, jumping from the bed.

He quickly threw on some pants, and went to the door. The handle was already too hot to touch. He protected his hand with a towel, and pulled the door open.

Heat and flames and smoke knocked Trumbull back a foot.

Eva dressed quickly and together they ran out past the growing flames, into the hallway.

She banged on doors. "Maria! Louisa! Freda!" The girls and an occasional 'John' ran out into the hallway, some of them still naked.

Screams and chaos marked the scene for several minutes until everyone made it outside into the street.

Trumbull, surrounded by half-clothed, scared girls, looked back at the building. The flames raced through the entire building now. A window from the second floor cracked and hot glass showered down onto the street.

Eva counted girls, and asked, "Where's Jessica?"

"Spent the night at Ray's," Louisa said.

One of the other girls panicking and taking quick, short, breaths asked, "Should we call the fire department?"

"I don't think the fire department is going to come," Trumbull said.

They all looked at Trumbull, and then followed his gaze down the block. The Key West Fire Chief was leaning against a building down the block, casually smoking, looking back at them. He looked bored. As they watched him, he threw his cigarette butt on the ground, and stepped on it with his boot. Then he turned and walked around the corner and out of sight.

ABSOLUTE POWER

As Trumbull drove back from the Keys, toward Miami, he thought about the money it cost to build the series of roadways for the drive. In 1950 the highway to Key West at times used damaged railroad trestles, where the railroad had been washed out by a hurricane. The road was built where the railroad once was.

"Dear Cuz;

Eva is not a bad woman. She runs a business, not a business most people approve of, though. People don't want to admit that there are prostitutes living and working among us. But Eva is a smart woman, knows how to run the business, and keep it running. All she has to do is pay kickbacks to Papy.

Eva decided she had had enough of paying kickbacks.

So they set fire to her business.

As they say; power corrupts, and absolute power corrupts absolutely.

Papy has absolute power in Key West."

Trumbull stopped his car where the shoulder was just wide enough to park away from the traffic. He slowly opened the car door and stepped out. He walked to the front of the car and stepped up to the guard rail. He looked out at the never-ending expanse of water, thinking. He was not thinking about anything in particular, He was just thinking.

Finally he got back into the driver's seat of the car, started the engine, and pulled out into the lane that would take him back to Miami.

Raised in the Ways of Righteousness

Murphy sat his desk typing. He was trying to type. Nothing seemed to be coming, though. He tried different sentences, typed two lines, looked at the paper in the typewriter, and tore it out of the machine, frustrated. The paper crumpled in his hand and joined a growing collection of crumpled papers in the nearby waste basket.

He took a blank sheet from the stack on the desk, fed it into the roller and twisted it into place.

He looked at the blank paper and dropped his head.

Trumbull stood around the corner watching him. Murphy was not aware that Trumbull had returned. Murphy rubbed his face with his hands and typed a few words. He stopped, looked at them, and typed a few more.

He twisted his face, and pulled the sheet out of the typewriter, crumpling it and tossing it into the waste basket.

"Having a bad day, Murphy?" Trumbull asked.

Murphy turned quickly, smiling at the sight of Trumbull.

"What gives you that idea?" Murphy asked.

Trumbull held a copy of the Herald in his hand. He held it up showing Murphy his story, buried on page 12. "Did Hills do this?" Trumbull asked, "Bury this story?"

"Don't remind me," Murphy said.

"He was right to bury it, Murphy."

"You have to twist the knife after it's already in my heart?"

Trumbull held the paper in his hands, adjusting it so he could read Murphy's story. "You have work to do," he said. "This Traynor –"

"Can't find him," Murphy said. "That's the whole problem. His office is empty."

"Is he hiding?" Trumbull asked. "Come on, he's elected. He'll turn up. It's just a matter of waiting, outlasting him."

"What do you want to do?" Murphy asked.

"Go to Tallahassee, you and me."

"I've turned over every rock, looked in every corner," Murphy said.

Trumbull looked at Murphy sideways. "Murphy, are you a journalist or not? Please don't tell me you're worn out on the best story we'll ever cover."

Murphy picked his head up. "Alright, let's go."

"Atta boy," Trumbull said.

They had left word with whoever was still in the office, with instructions to tell Hills first thing in the morning. And then they were driving.

Trumbull was at the wheel and Murphy watched the world pass by from the passenger seat.

When they arrived in Tallahassee they wasted no time getting to work. Trumbull instructed Murphy to blanket the State House building with as many questions as he could ask, while Trumbull himself took on the job of tracking down the truant, Representative Traynor.

Murphy did a good enough job. He didn't expect to learn anything he didn't already know, but he did uncover one or two hidden critics of Papy. They didn't have anything illegal to report; stories of veiled threats, unspoken promises slipped into conversations from cronies. It was interesting stuff, though, so Murphy took meticulous notes.

Trumbull had checked Traynor's assigned - and empty - office. He had to admit Murphy had indeed done his job, so he began asking around among colleagues. No one seemed to know where Traynor worked.

Finally after several hours of hunting and turning up nothing, he re-united with Murphy, and went over Murphy's new notes.

They were interesting, sure - another page 12 story. But they didn't drive all the way up from Miami for a page 12 story. So Trumbull sighed and said, "One more check before we head in for the night."

Together Trumbull and Murphy walked the long corridors to the familiar row of offices. They were tired, but determined to see this through. They turned the corner leading to Traynor's designated office, and were very surprised to find the door standing open.

Inside the office stood a man six feet tall, skinny, wearing a clean pressed suit and bow tie. Surrounding him were several newly unpacked boxes of papers, books, and odds and ends.

"Excuse me," Trumbull said.

"Yes?" said the skinny man.

"I'm looking for Representative Traynor."

"That's me," the skinny man said.

Trumbull walked into the office followed by Murphy. Neither man could believe their luck. "We're from the Miami Herald," Trumbull said.

Murphy cleared his throat, and added, "You don't answer your phone, Mr. Traynor."

"I don't actually have a telephone in this office yet," the young Representative said. "I'm just moving in, you see."

"Mr. Traynor, you've been elected for some time now, as I understand it," Trumbull said, carefully choosing his words. "Where have you been working?"

"My mother – " Traynor trailed off, coughed, and looked at the two reporters. There was fear in his eyes. "She didn't want me to be in this building at first."

"Your mother?" Trumbull looked at Murphy, barely concealing his disbelief.

"She's coming tomorrow to be my secretary," Traynor said.

Trumbull realized he had the man on his hook, and decided he better get the basics out of the way before he wriggled free. "Is it alright if we ask you a few questions?"

Representative Traynor shifted slightly on his feet. "Where did you say you're from?"

"The Miami Herald."

"Well, I suppose it would be alright," Traynor said.

Trumbull flipped his notebook open. "Now let's see," he said, "Representative Traynor, Mr. Papy has been overheard, by my colleague Murphy here, telling a story about you. He told other representatives that he shook your hand and tried to squeeze money into it. Can you confirm that the story is true?"

The color ran out of Traynor's face. He shook slightly. His voice broke a little as he said, "I was raised in the ways of righteousness. I took an oath of office and strive to do only what is right in this world. I am legally barred from accepting any gratuity or – "

Trumbull cut him off. "Yes, yes, Mr. Traynor, can you just confirm for us that the story is true?"

"A month ago I would not have thought it possible," Traynor said.

Trumbull's patience – what little of it that had ever existed – was worn thin. "Representative Traynor, was Papy trying to buy your vote?"

Traynor was silent. He looked down, then said, "Yes," almost too faintly to hear. "I haven't told my mother."

"Thank you," Trumbull said. "Next question – "

Outside, moments later, Trumbull and Murphy could not hold their laughter. "Good Lord almighty," Trumbull chortled.

"What a sap," added Murphy.

"That man needs whiskey and a hooker, bad."

"At least he's credible," Murphy said. "He's a source, and a good one."

Finally, after a very long day, Trumbull decided it was time to find a good Tallahassee bar. He didn't really know the town, but he was sure as hell going to find someplace with a good single malt before checking into a local hotel.

He pulled up to a small but respectable looking place, and he and Murphy went in for their first relaxing moment all day.

Knocking on Doors

Editor Hills was sitting at his desk going over copy for the next day's front page, when his Secretary, Betsy, came in unannounced.

"Mr. Hills, there's a gentleman here to see you," she said.

Hills took his feet down from the top of the desk and looked at Betsy questioningly. He noticed a slight agitation in Betsy, and knew that whoever it was had shaken up his usually trustworthy Secretary.

But before he could ask who it was, Mr. Davis, Papy's right hand man, came boldly through the door. "Editor Hills, a word, please," he said. And then in a moment of presumptiveness that annoyed Hills, he turned to Betsy and added, "Thank you. That will be all."

"Excuse me," Hills said, rising from his chair. "She's my secretary. I did not tell her I had time to meet with you."

"I'm Gordon Davis, Representative Bernie Papy's aide."

"I'm sure that makes you feel very important. How lucky for you that you can throw Papy's weight around like that. Fortunately for you, Mr. Davis, I'm in a good mood. I'll meet with you, but next time you'll have to get Betsy's approval. And I particularly like it when Betsy tells people 'no.'" Hills then turned to Betsy and calmly told her, "alright, you can go."

Davis hardly waited for the secretary to leave before driving the conversation forward. "Mr. Hills," he said, "I want to discuss with you the matter of your paper assassinating the character of Representative Papy."

"Mr. Davis, please sit down," said Hills. "It is time for me to educate you."

"If you don't mind, I prefer to stand."

"Sit down!"

Davis stared blankly at Hills. He had not expected this. Slowly, under Hills surprisingly authoritative gaze, Davis backed into the chair behind him and sat.

"My paper, Mr. Davis, is not assassinating anyone's character." Hills remained standing looking down toward Davis. "We are reporting the news. Your boss, Papy, has no respect for news. News is truth. Men like him have no use for truth. Truth has this nasty habit of muddling his opinions all up."

"This witch hunt is getting out of control," Davis said.

"'Witch hunt,' that's an interesting way of putting it," Hills said. "I've heard Papy use that phrase himself. I suppose it has a nice scandalous ring to it."

"Your reporters are harassing people," Davis said.

"Harassing?" Hills paused for a moment, smiling broadly at Davis. "What are they doing that you consider harassing?"

"They're asking people questions," Davis said meekly.

"Oh! Dear me!" Hills shouted. "My reporters are asking people questions!"

"They're knocking on people's doors," Davis continued. "They're stopping people in the hallway, asking them what they know."

Hills could no longer keep a straight face. "Are you complaining to me that my reporters are knocking on people's doors? Asking them things?"

"It's very disruptive," Davis said.

"They're knocking on doors!" Hills let out a laugh, and then did his best to speak seriously. "Mr. Davis, I'm shocked. I can't believe that Trumbull would actually knock on a door before he opens it." He laughed again and spoke quietly. "It's touching really. It might be the nicest thing anyone's said about Trumbull in years." At this point Hills changed to a very serious tone of voice and barked, "Now get out of my office and go back to your own little world."

Defeated, Davis rose from the chair. He acted like he was about to speak, but when nothing came, Hills filled the void.

"Knocking on doors!" he said, laughing again.

Davis turned to the door and quietly left.

EXPECTED BETTER FROM YOU

Eva sat alone at a table in The Boat Bar. The happy world of gaming went on around her, but she tuned it out. She didn't find any pleasure in it tonight. She had barely slept for two days, and wanted to be left alone.

She raised her glass to her lips and sipped her drink as Martins sat at the table next to her. She didn't look up. She knew it was Martins from the same jacket, pants and shoes he always wore. She turned away to avoid looking at him.

"I had a job to do, Eva," he said.

She let this sentence hang quietly on its own for a moment. Finally she found herself responding.

"I expected better from you," she said.

"You liked him, didn't you," Martins said.

"Who," she asked.

"Trumbull."

"I don't get involved with men," she said.

"Seems to me you spend just about all your time getting involved with men."

She took another drink and finally looked at him. "You shook me down, you played me."

"Look Eva," Martins said, "we're not shutting you down for good."

Eva was at a loss. She didn't know how to talk to him anymore, so she laughed. "Have you seen the building?" she asked. "You did shut me down for good."

Martins looked her in the eye. "I have a proposal for you, Eva."

"I'm not interested."

"Hear me out."

"You can talk. I'm not interested, though."

Martins did his best to show her he was sincere. He put his elbows on the table and held his hands together in front of her. "I didn't want to do it," he said. "I didn't want to shake you down or burn your building."

Eva wasn't buying it. "That's touching," she said. "What's the punch line?"

"It's Papy, Eva. It's Papy."

"Okay." She looked at him, half convinced. "And?"

Martins spoke quietly, darting his eyes around the room first, to make sure no one could overhear. "I think your reporter friend is right."

Eva held her position. She was reading Martin's face for any signs of lying. "What are you suggesting?" She asked.

HOOKING THE SHARK

Hills sat at the head of the large conference room table. His feet were up, as usual. He focused intently on the papers in his hands.

Around the corner of the table to his right sat Murphy. To his left, Trumbull sat calmly.

None of them spoke while Hills read through the story. Trumbull and Murphy looked at each other. Murphy decided to copy Trumbull's calm demeanor. Finally Hills broke the silence.

"How solid is this?"

It's solid," Trumbull said. "He's on record. He even said he'd testify in court."

Hills rubbed his face with his hands and looked up. "Papy's aide, Gordon Davis, was in here yesterday. He accused you guys of knocking on doors."

Trumbull smiled slightly. "Sorry," he said. "It won't happen again."

Hills took his feet down, and scooted closer to the table. "Tell me something. Answer this question for me; are we reporting the news, or are we making the news?"

"This is bigger than us, Hills," Trumbull said. "It's happening. We're reporting it."

"We are about to run a story accusing a State Representative of buying votes. Have you thought about involving the FBI in your story?"

Murphy looked across at Trumbull. He wanted to speak, but stopped himself. Trumbull motioned to him to go ahead.

"I understand why you're asking," Murphy said, "but this story is coming directly from the accusers now. Why don't we run the story first, and see how the FBI responds after its public?"

Hills sat for a moment, thoughtful, ruminating. "No," he said, "To be a complete story, you need to call the FBI, tell them we are running a story in which credible sources accuse Papy of buying votes, and would they care to comment?"

"He's right, Murphy," Trumbull said. "It's better to have a line that says, 'The FBI declined to comment,' than to have no mention at all."

"This is a legal issue," continued Hills. "This is something that could put Papy behind bars. We're not just reporting that cops stopped a car on the street. We're reporting that an elected official is breaking the law, and here's our proof."

"You're worried, aren't you, Hills." Trumbull said.

Hills took a moment before responding. "Papy has pretty good cards. We have to admit that. Who do we know in the FBI?"

"I know Douglas, in Jacksonville a little," Murphy said.

"And what if Papy has Douglas in Jacksonville in his own back pocket?" Hills asked.

Trumbull calmly looked up, and said, "I'll call Washington. I have a source."

"You have a source?"

Trumbull eyed Hills steadily. "I have a source," he repeated.

Hills exhaled and sat back in his chair. He looked up at the ceiling for a minute, thinking, then turned back to Trumbull. "Okay, call Washington. Are we just getting a comment, or are we passing information to the FBI that we hope they'll run with?"

"Does it matter?" Trumbull asked.

Hills eyed Trumbull the way Trumbull had been eyeing him. "Let me spell it out this way, gentlemen," he said, "this is hooking the shark. You know what I mean? If you're going to pull the shark out of the water, into your boat, you better know for certain that you can kill the shark."

Bring Trumbull down

The man had Prescott by his shirt collar. He dragged Prescott into the bathroom and pushed his back up against the wall. Prescott gasped. He whimpered slightly, but did not resist.

Papy walked into the room.

The man held Prescott against the wall, as Papy walked slowly toward them. Prescott's breathing increased rapidly.

"Damn it, Prescott," Papy said. "I LIKE you."

"I swear, Papy, I'll get the money," bleated Prescott.

"I'm tired of your promises."

Prescott wanted the man's hand to move away from his neck. He could not breathe. A quick tussle took place, as Prescott tried to shift and the man threw him back against the wall.

"Come on," Prescott pleaded. "I...I..."

Papy shook his head. "I promise. I promise. I promise. It's the same thing over and over."

"Just give me until tomorrow," Prescott said.

Papy waved the man away, and stood directly in front of Prescott. He adopted his friendly, familial demeanor and patted Prescott's face with his hand. "Prescott, Prescott," he said warmly. "Do you have any idea how much it hurts me to do this to you? You are a friend. I care about you."

"Papy please-"

"You're like a brother to me," Papy went on. "But you know what? Sometimes brothers go astray. Sometimes brothers need a little bit of motivation."

Prescott tried to be as calm and confident as he could. "I - I see you as a brother, too," he said hopefully, trying to smile at Papy.

Papy didn't appreciate the attempt. He shifted his feet and continued. "You even shot one of our birds. That bird was named 'Patton.' I named that bird. 'Patton' was my bird."

The door to the bathroom burst open behind them and Davis entered the room urgently.

Papy looked at Davis. He did not like the interruption. "Davis, this better be important," he said.

"It's important," Davis said. "I need a word with you."

Papy recognized the urgency in Davis' voice, and said, "Let's talk out here," motioning Davis out toward the hallway.

The two men exited the bathroom and walked to a quiet corner of the hallway, where they spoke in hushed tones.

"I just got a call from Douglas." Davis waited for a note of recognition from Papy. None came. "Douglas, Jacksonville....FBI."

Papy nodded, "Right. Douglas, FBI."

"Trumbull put in a call to someone in Washington,"

"And...?" Papy wasn't sure where this was leading.

"The Herald is running a story about buying votes. Trumbull called the FBI. They're moving on this."

Papy thought quickly. "Can Douglas put a lid on it?" he asked.

"He sounded worried."

"Small-minded people," Papy said absently. "Okay, call Henderson. Tell him we need him."

"On it," Davis said.

"Handle this, Davis."

"I'll handle it."

Papy turned to leave, turned back around and faced Davis. "Trumbull has gone as far as he is going to go," he said angrily. "It's time we bring him down."

"What exactly are you telling me to do?" Davis asked.

"What did I just say?" Papy looked at Davis without flinching. "I said it's time to bring Trumbull down."

Papy turned away from Davis and walked back toward the bathroom door.

Beat Him at His Own Game

"Dear Cuz;

I am on my way back to Key West. I know, burned once, burned twice, I've heard all the warnings. But I have a little unfinished business to take care of.

You see Cuz, it's one thing to expose Papy's corrupt control of this town. The ultimate revenge, though, comes when I beat him at his own game."

Trumbull had made the drive back to Key West, and entered The Boat Bar with a new lightness in his step. On his way to the bar, he turned to the poker table and shouted, "Gentlemen, I would like to join your game." Then he slapped a Twenty on the bar, and told the bartender, "You aren't out. I can see the bottle. Give me the good stuff. Do it."

The bartender smiled a wry smile, took the twenty, and reached for the bottle on the top shelf.

Within minutes, Trumbull had already won his first hand, annoying the regulars and drawing the attention of several spectators.

Meanwhile, back in Miami, the Herald printing room buzzed with the usual late-night whirring of the massive printing press. Thousands of copies of the next morning's paper spun through the press and landed on a massive slab of concrete, where they were folded, stacked, and prepared for their early morning delivery.

At the poker table, Trumbull showed he was something of a master.

"Raise," he said, hiding his cards and his emotions equally well.

To his right, a man wearing a beat up hat, who Trumbull recognized from previous games, looked Trumbull in the eye, trying to read him. "Call," the man said.

Across the table a player lost faith in his hand and folded.

Now there remained only Trumbull and the man in the beat up hat. The dealer dealt each player their final card. Trumbull took his card and, keeping his face down, considered his options. He looked up at the man in the beat up hat, and proceeded to push his chips toward the center of the table.

The man looked at the new stack of chips. He looked at Trumbull.

Several hours drive away, Papy, Davis, and other familiar faces were also on their way to Key West. The mood in the car was serious.

Editor Lee Hills had finished his work for the day and decided to check in at the printing room before going home. It was late. He had worked a long day.

As he entered the loud room, one of the workers, who Hills had known for several years now, nodded to him, held up the front page. "Hell of story this time," the man said.

Hills smiled and nodded at the man. He looked out at the large spinning press, copies of the next morning's Herald rolling through the printer. Hills knew he had done a good job today. He felt good.

At The Boat Bar, the crowd of spectators had grown. Eva watched from behind Trumbull. Time slowed down for her. She thought about what might have been, what never could be. For a moment, in the silence, as the man in the beat up hat considered what play to make, you could almost hear Eva's heart beat, as she watched Trumbull from behind.

"I gotta fold," the man in the beat up hat finally said, throwing his cards on the table.

Trumbull had won. Now all eyes were on his cards. Was he bluffing or not? Trumbull looked around the room, realizing for the first time the number of spectators who had been watching. He looked at the man in the beat up hat, and smiled. He took a swig of his drink and turned his cards over. A lousy busted straight.

"I knew you were bluffing!" The man in the beat up hat said. "God damn!"

Trumbull stood and began collecting his winnings. The crowd, impressed, slowly began to disperse.

Eva walked up to Trumbull as he put the last of his winnings in his coat pocket. "How's business?" he asked.

"I'm out of business," Eva said. "How's yours? How's the newspaper life?"

"It's the only life," Trumbull said, "the only business. What are you going to do? Stay? Leave town?"

"I have family in Havana," said Eva.

They had begun walking toward the door, but a familiar face now stood in front of them.

"Hello Walter," Trumbull said.

"Mr. Trumbull."

"You're a gentleman, Walter, coming to say good bye."

Walter looked out from under the brim of his hat. "I hope, Mr. Trumbull, that you had an enjoyable time. You certainly seemed to enjoy collecting your winnings."

Trumbull, who was full of unusual smiles tonight, said, "If I didn't know better, I would suspect that gambling is going on here."

"Before you go," Walter said. "We have a little rule here at The Boat Bar."

In an instant all traces of a smile were gone from Trumbull's face. "I don't much care for your rules, Walter," he said. "Come on, Eva. Let's get out of this place."

As Trumbull took Eva's arm, and began moving toward the door, Key West's favorite two goons stepped in their path.

Trumbull knew the goon's moves, now. He had observed their tendencies, and in a quick movement he grabbed one of the goon's guns from it's hidden pocket, and shoved the goon up against the door, the gun pointed at the goon's belly.

"It's alright," Trumbull said. "I'm in a good mood, from all the winning I've been part of tonight." Trumbull pulled the gun up, un-cocked it, and put it in his own pocket.

"Good night. It was a pleasure," he said, shoving the goons aside and leading Eva out the door.

Outside, Eva and Trumbull walked quickly to the corner and down a side street. Trumbull was pretty sure they would not be followed tonight, but he also felt a need to get out of sight quickly.

Eva told him to follow her to her hotel room, instead of going to the hotel that he had checked into. She led him down a second side street, into the lobby of a modest, unpretentious building, and up a flight of stairs. They walked down a short hallway, and she pulled out a key as they approached room 212. She turned the key in the lock, opened the door, and turned on the light. Sitting on Eva's bed – waiting for who-knows-how-long in the dark – was Key West's finest, Police Chief Darrel Martins. He looked up at Trumbull and Eva and squinted as the light flooded the room.

"What's this, Eva?" Trumbull asked. "I know Key West has a broad minded reputation, but it's not quite my style."

Martins looked at Eva and asked, "Did you tell him?"

"Not yet," she said.

There was an awkward silence.

"Someone please tell me," Trumbull said.

Martins began, speaking quietly. "You know how dangerous it is for me to be seen with you?"

"It might suggest to people that you're raising your standards," Trumbull said.

"Eva and I have decided we're ready to tell the truth."

Trumbull twisted his head a little, wondering whether to believe him. "What was it that caused you to make this decision?"

"Eventually everyone reaches their breaking point, "Martins said.

"You're saying you'll go on record with me?" Trumbull asked. "I can use your name?"

"I need some help," Martins said. "My life will be in serious danger. Is there anything you can do to protect me?"

"Well," Trumbull ruminated for a moment. "The paper can't do anything to protect you from Papy. We're just a newspaper. We could run a story about you being afraid for your life, maybe. But let's say there was legal action. Let's imagine maybe the FBI was involved. Would you be willing to cooperate with them?"

"Yes," Martins said emphatically.

"You'll be alright, Martins. Papy's small-time. He's amateur-hour. You've made the right decision. The FBI should be here by morning."

"Okay, okay," Martins said. He stood up. "For tonight, I never spoke to you. I don't even know you came back to town."

"Good night, Martins," Trumbull said. "I hope Papy enjoys the morning paper."

YOU AND ME

Key West awoke the next morning to its usual idyllic soundtrack. The surf slowly lapped up against the docks, rocking fishing boats at their moorage ever so slightly. Seagulls wailed, gliding on the wind across the water, in search of small fish to sneak up on.

Somewhere an all-night poker game finally ended, and a handful of drunk, sleep-deprived men stumbled outdoors, squinting awkwardly as the morning sun bathed the community in its warm glow.

A rag tag collection of hard-working 12-year-old boys gathered at the local newspaper distribution center. A few of them would load up bicycle bags and head out on a paper route. The rest would set up on key street corners.

They added their own chorus to the seagulls and the lazy, rhythmic, lapping of the ocean waves.

"Paper! Paper! Representative Papy trying to buy votes! Paper!"

Papy himself had risen early this morning. He felt good about things — cocky, actually. He was walking from one of his local residences - a donated suite in the city's finest hotel - to the police station, when he heard the chorus. He turned toward a boy standing opposite him, across the street.

"Papy buying votes in state government! Read all about it!" the boy shouted.

Papy turned to the two cronies walking with him, and frowned. Together the men stepped out in the street, disregarding traffic, and causing several cars to slam their brakes.

As they approached the boy, he looked directly at Papy unaware of who Papy was and yelled, "Corrupt state government! Paper!"

"Hey, hey, boy," Papy said.

"Paper, sir, read all ab-"

"How many do you have there?" Papy asked.

"Huh?"

"How many do you have left?"

The boy twisted his face in confusion, and looked at the papers next to him. "I don't know," he said, "twenty five?"

Papy pulled out a Twenty. "Give them to me."

"All of them?"

"All of them," Papy said. "Hand them over."

The boy reached for the Twenty. "Thanks," he said.

"Go play with your friends," said Papy.

"Okay."

After the boy ran off, Papy and his cronies stood on the street corner, squinting, scanning the blocks for more paper boys.

It was at about this same time, several miles away, that a group of unmarked black sedans left the mainland, and edged out onto the 110-mile long Overseas Highway that would lead them eventually to Key West.

And it was also around this time, in the early morning, that Trumbull was on the phone with his editor, Lee Hills. He was explaining to Hills that he was fairly sure Martins was telling the truth, that they could add Martins to the list of people they could name as sources against Papy.

Hills was full of questions, of course. He was a good editor, and good editors never stop asking questions. Trumbull assured him he would proceed cautiously.

"And don't do anything that could put you in the hospital," Hills said.

"Got it, Hills," Trumbull said, before hanging up.

Trumbull sat in a rustic wooden chair facing the window. He didn't move for a few minutes, until he heard Eva rustling in the bed behind him. He turned and saw that her eyes were open. She was barely covered by the thin bed sheet. She was naked.

"You should put some clothes on," Trumbull said. "This is going to be a very interesting day."

She didn't move. She stared at Trumbull, thinking about something much different than what he was thinking about. Trumbull looked back at her. Finally she sat up in the bed.

"I don't get something," she said.

"What don't you get?"

"You and me."

Trumbull looked away. "There's nothing to get."

"I don't know..." she said, trailing off the unfinished thought.

"Is this how you plan to make me fall in love with you?" Trumbull asked. "Lying there naked, talking about 'you and me'?"

"You're a cold man, Trumbull," Eva said.

He didn't respond at first. He thought about the way things had ended with Sarah. He preferred not to revisit those days, but something about Eva made him think about the god-forsaken story. Should he tell her? No, he thought. No need.

The final three months with Sarah had turned into a manic depressive seesaw, for both Sarah and Trumbull. He almost kicked her out at the first sign of trouble, but somehow she came down from that wild manic episode and convinced him it would not happen again.

Then it began happening every few weeks, then every week, then every few days. She accused him of things, crazy things. He wasn't sure where she came up with some of her ideas.

When she came at him with a pair of scissors, screaming obscenities at him, stabbing violently into thin air, after he restrained her arms, he felt something break inside him.

He had no choice but to turn her over to the police.

Three policemen hand cuffed her and took her away, as she continued a monologue of threats and curses that hung in the air of the apartment for weeks afterwards. He moved out, to get away from the memories. He took an apartment on the other side of town. He buried himself in work. Eventually he found his way in life again, and it didn't seem to include women.

He felt okay with that.

Sitting in the chair, Trumbull turned to Eva again. She looked nearly perfect; her naked body looked like that of an experienced Venus. She had just the right amount of lines on her face, lines that said she was no longer a girl, that she had lived through enough to understand a thing or two.

"Eva," he said.

"Yes?"

"If it helps any," he paused and looked her in the eye, "I'll remember you."

She looked at him, unable to think or move.

"I'll remember only good things," he said. "It's all good things."

CHANGE OF PLANS

There was a sort of summit going on at the Police Headquarters. Martins was there. Davis was there. A handful of the other Papy cronies were there. Most important, Papy was there, and he wasn't happy.

"We should have – no, we COULD have stopped this before it went this far," he said. He had been talking for a good twenty minutes. He was holding court. No one else got a word in, and in truth, no one tried. "So, what is our next step? What are our next steps? I need a clear plan of action."

He looked expectantly at the men who did his dirty work. No one said a thing.

Eventually the awkward silence was too much for Papy, and he grabbed a clip board from the nearby desk and hurled it at the men. Davis ducked to his left. Martins threw his hands in the way, but the clip board sailed past him, and cut the forehead of the man behind him.

"Jeezus, Bernie!" the man said, dabbing at the fresh blood before running into a nearby bathroom.

Finally it was Martins who broke the awkward silence. "We have to expand our influence," he said. "We may not have any influence over the Washington FBI boys, but that's just a temporary problem, right?"

"Right," agreed Davis. "They're men, just like here. We offer them the right incentives, these things can get taken care of."

Papy began to breathe easier. "And we need to take care of Trumbull and Eva," he said.

"And it has to be clean." It was Martins again, agreeing with Papy's intention to end that particular problem.

"Clean," Papy said. "It has to be perfect. What ideas do you have?"

"We do what we did with Scooter Blivens," Martins said. Everyone agreed. Scooter was the most successful disappearance in years. One day he was stopped on the street by men no one recognized, hustled into a black car, and driven away. No one ever saw or heard from him again. The case remained unsolved. No one was ever charged.

"Scooter," Papy said, a hint of a smile creeping across his face. "What ever happened to him anyway?" Everyone laughed. "Alright," Papy said, "Do it right. Keep it squeaky clean."

"Actually," Martins said, looking out the window, "I think we may have a change of plans."

The entourage of FBI cars had arrived. They were lined up outside the Police Headquarters, side by side, a gauntlet awaiting a confrontation. Agent Baker was the man in charge. He strode confidently behind the cars barking out orders. "Jackson, Struggs, keep your men in line. No one trigger happy, okay."

Inside, Papy followed Martins' gaze through the window. "Away from the window!" Papy ordered. Everyone stepped back. They hid around a hallway corner. "Why are they here?"Papy asked.

No one answered. Papy looked at Martins. Nervously, Martins said, "Has to be Trumbull. Heard a rumor he was back in town last night."

"But how would they know to come here?" Papy asked, a tone of suspicion creeping into his questions.

Martins coughed and thought quickly. "You were out this morning. You haven't been discreet. People have seen you."

When Martins finished, Papy's look had changed. Looking down, Martins saw the glint of a gun barrel poking out from behind Papy's jacket.

"You double-crossing Judas," Papy said. "You think I don't know? You've been talking to Eva."

"What? What are you talking about?" Martins said, pleadingly.

Papy shoved the gun barrel into Martins chest. "Do you really think you can play dumb with me? Martins, I know everything that's worth knowing in this town. You think it's just you and Walter? I have ears in every room in this town."

"Okay, okay," Martins admitted. "I talked to her. Of course I talked to her. She's angry."

"You're a turncoat, Martins," Papy said, bringing the gun up to his face.

"This is ridiculous, "Martins said. "Papy you've lost your mind. Put the gun down."

Papy ignored him. "You're going to go out there," Papy said. "You're going to go out and talk to the FBI, and tell them I went back to the mainland this morning." Papy tapped the business end of the gun barrel on Martins cheek. "You're going to do what I tell you, Martins. And if you don't, I'll let the FBI know everything about you, everything I know — everything. I'll even give them a solution to the Scooter Blivens case that I think they're going to like."

"What good does this do?" Martin asked. "So I tell them you went back to the mainland. They'll find you eventually. What then?"

"All this time, and you haven't learned a damn thing," Papy said. "Time, Martins, TIME. That's all I need. That's all I ever need. Given enough time, any problem can be solved. Give me enough time, and I'll have the goddamn

Washington FBI bureau chief in my pocket. Now get out there and start telling them I drove back to the mainland. If anyone asks when, I left about an hour ago."

The two men looked eyeball to eyeball. Martins backed up a step. Slowly, Martins turned toward the door. He walked to it, turned the handle and opened it.

Outside, Martins held out his police badge. He closed the door to the station behind him, and held the badge up in the air. "It's alright!" He shouted. "I am Key West Police Chief Darrel Martins."

"Easy, men!" Baker yelled out from behind one of the cars.

"I'm cooperating!" Martins shouted.

He stood halfway between the cars and the station, hands in the air, Police badge raised high. Carefully, Baker stepped out from behind the car, and approached him.

"Where is Florida State Representative Bernard Papy?" Baker asked.

Martins looked at the FBI agent for a moment before answering. A smile crept across his lips. "He's inside," Martins said. "I'm the one who called it in. Better surround the building. There's a back door. He's probably heading for it right now."

"He's inside?" Baker asked.

"He's inside," Martins confirmed.

It took ten minutes, but eventually Papy was dragged out of the Police Station, literally kicking and screaming.

Trumbull and Eva had arrived to watch the show. Martins was talking to FBI Agent Baker about provisions for protecting his life, given the potential danger Martins was now placing himself in.

As Papy was dragged past Martins, a free-form, almost poetic stream of obscenities chorused down the block.

"Martins you are a tiny little piece of carpet lint. I should just vacuum you up and throw you out with the rotting food and the stinking fish and the, the fleas and the mongrel dogs that eat you. You're nothing more than - And you too Trumbull! You dirty little, little... WRITER! You think you can just sit with your, your, PEN and, and, and your, your typewriter, and WRITE things! And you too, Eva! All three of you! Didn't nobody ever teach you how to-"

A car door slammed shut on him, and nobody heard the rest of the speech.

Trumbull pulled his flask from his coat pocket. He tipped it back and smiled. "That's what I like to see," Trumbull said, "Papy handcuffed, rambling on and on like a crazy man."

The car with Papy inside started up. FBI agents were getting into their cars. They began pulling out. Martins and Baker shook hands, and Martins got in behind Baker, as the remaining car engines started. One by one they pulled away.

Trumbull and Eva watched them drive off into the distance.

As they began walking, Eva looked over at Trumbull. She did not want to face this moment. "Trumbull," she said.

"Eva, there's no need to say anything."

"You're going back to Miami," she said. "I'll stay her just long enough to testify. Then I leave for Havana."

"Havana," Trumbull said, reflectively. "I'm jealous."

"I want to apologize," Eva said.

Trumbull stopped walking and turned to her. "Eva," he said, "men like me aren't made for relationships."

"Especially with women like me."

"With anyone," he said. He wanted to tell her how wrong she was, in singling herself out, but held his tongue.

"I guess women like me aren't made for relationships either," she said.

"Maybe that makes us perfect for each other," Trumbull replied.

"Who would have thought we'd be so perfect?"

"I'm going to miss you, Eva," he said.

"That's almost romantic of you to say. I'll miss you too, Stephen."

"You can't resist, can you."

"Sorry."

They looked into each other's eyes for a moment longer. Finally, in silence, Trumbull turned away. Eva watched him as he walked, his back to her, wondering if he would turn back one more time, at least to wave, if not to say anything more. He never turned back. She called after him.

"If you ever make it to Havana," she said.

Trumbull turned. "Maybe I will," he said. "Hemingway lives there now."

They shared one last lingering look, and then Trumbull turned away for good.

Damn Good Newspapermen

The next morning, paper boys across Florida sang a chorus in near unison. In Key West, in Miami, in Tampa, in Tallahassee, they echoed the cry of the boy across the street from the Herald offices; "Paper! Paper! Papy arrested! Read all about it!"

Trumbull, Hills, and Murphy weren't awake to hear it that morning, though. After all the struggle, the strategizing, and the hand wringing, they celebrated their journalistic feat with a little too much drinking, and a few too many late-night hours before sleeping.

They stayed up at Trumbull's favorite spot. It began innocently enough, but eventually even the usually responsible Hills relaxed and gave in to the moment.

"Feels good," Trumbull said, "feels real damn good."

Hills raised his glass. "To Papy," he said.

"To Papy," echoed Murphy.

"To Papy," said Trumbull. "May he always land on his ass!"

The three men drank and slapped each other on the back. Hills set his empty glass on the bar and turned to his left. "Trumbull," he said.

"Yes?"

"I have just one request for the future."

"Here it comes," Trumbull said, rolling his eyes.

"In the future," Hills began, "do you think you could avoid taking on stories that might KILL you?"

"I'm alive, aren't I," Trumbull responded.

"Barely," Hills muttered.

Trumbull turned to Murphy and casually raised his glass again. "Murphy, I have a lot more respect for you these days. You're a damn good newspaperman."

Hills barked out, "We're all damn good newspapermen."

Murphy, who had been drinking the same amount as Hills and Trumbull, was feeling the effects more intensely than either of the other two. "Everything I know," he said, noticeably unsure of himself, " I learned from you, Trumple."

"Matt," Trumbull shouted at the bartender. "Give this man another drink."

"No, no," Murphy protested.

But Matt was more accustomed to granting Trumbull's wishes than Murphy's, and before Murphy could stage a full protest, a glass stood invitingly in front of him. Murphy took it, raised it, and said, "To the pen being mightier than the sword!"

"No, Murphy," Trumbull said, "you see, it's all about using the pen AS a sword."

"You mean you could possibly have a sword fight with a pen?"

"I've done it many times," said Trumbull.

"Do you have to wear the thing?" Murphy was now on the verge of becoming disjointed and incoherent. "You know, the thing, they wear the fencing thing, the, the-"

"Murphy, you're drunk!" Trumbull proclaimed.

"Ssssslander! Lies, and innnnn – yu – endo!"

The Rest of the Story

The Miami Herald won the Pulitzer Prize in 1951, for crime reporting. Much of the credit goes to their investigations into State Representative Bernie Papy.

As is often the case in real life, though, that was hardly the end of the story. It is not an easy thing to report, here, as heroic as this story was, but Papy eventually beat those vote-buying charges.

He beat them. That's the truth, and Trumbull would be disappointed if this book ended with any other, less truthful impression.

Papy continued in the Florida State House, getting re-elected for twelve more years, until the voters of Monroe County finally voted him out in 1962. That year Trumbull wrote a column explaining that so complete and far-reaching was Papy's power network, that even out of office Papy would still be calling the shots. He counted the "Papy-votes," against the "non-Papy-votes" and explained that Papy no longer needed to vote or hold official office in order to control the fate of many issues.

Two years after that, cancer did what no human could do. It defeated Papy.

Under pressure from the Navy, the FBI eventually began a series of sweeps to clean illegal gambling out of Key West. It wasn't easy. The locals were always uncooperative.

The same refrain was heard time and again; "In Key West, the rules are just different." Long after Papy was gone, Key West continued to operate under a different set of rules than anywhere else.

In 1973, Florida Governor Reuben Askew asked the Broward State Attorney's office to follow up on a thick folder full of legal complaints relating to Key West. A seemingly true story recounts that the investigating team of attorneys found limburger cheese smeared into the air conditioners of their motel rooms.

Two years after that, Key West's most famous unsolved disappearance occurred. Fire Chief Joseph "Bum" Farto – that's his real honest-to-god name – was hustled into a car by strangers and driven away. That was the last anyone ever saw or heard from him. Key West's patron saint, Jimmy Buffet often wore "Where is Bum Farto?" t-shirts at his concerts. There is a rumor that suggests Bum Farto had been selling drugs out of the Key West Fire Station, and had probably undercut someone else's drug territory.

Out-in-the-open gambling was finally cleaned up, and the off-shore gambling boat industry sprouted up in its place.

You may remember those three clueless tourists trying to make it to the Lady Luck during that hurricane. As you may have guessed already, hurricanes were the undoing of that industry. After The Lady Luck suffered it's near-destruction in 2005, it was grounded for years and eventually the tables and machines were stolen.

These days the rules have loosened up a little, and it isn't hard to find places where you can gamble legally. Like Trumbull said, though, gambling isn't the problem. Hypocrisy and corruption are.

In 2006 a secretive group was discovered and infiltrated, and eight roosters, all with the tell-tale signs of being prepped for cock-fights (combs, wattles and saddle feathers removed) were discovered. The people were arrested and the birds taken away.

In 2007, while building condominiums on a block of Old Town Key West, a construction worker found a loaded hand gun buried in the dirt. No one could be sure, because the Boat Bar had been gone for years, but some asked the question, was this where the Boat Bar's old back door was?

I suppose these days Key West is most famous for its cross-dressing, gender-bending New Year's Eve Party. Some might think that marks a change for Key West. But I see that, and I think about a place where rules have always had a life of their own, a place where anything and everything, every deviation from "normal" society, has always found a way to indulge itself, and I think; well, why the hell not?

THE END

ABOUT THE AUTHOR

Peter Wick is an award-winning independent filmmaker and writer. He has Produced, Written, Directed, and Acted in three independent feature films, all with the support of grants from Seattle non-profit, Northwest Film Forum. All three films have won film festival awards. Most recently Peter won "Best Director" at the New York International Film Festival in 2011, for his feature, "Rock Paper Scissors." He has also performed stand-up comedy at clubs around the United States. "Key West" is his first novel. He currently lives in Los Angeles, California

Peter can be followed on Twitter: @juventinopw

You may also visit his website: www.peter-wick.com

www.ingramcontent.com/pod-product-compliance
Lightning Source LLC
Chambersburg PA
CBHW032043290426
44110CB00012B/924